POLLY CLARKSON

# BEATING
# THE
# BULLIES

Twenty Inspiring True-Life Stories of Triumph over
Violence, Intimidation and Bullying

JOHN BLAKE

Published by John Blake Publishing Ltd,
3 Bramber Court, 2 Bramber Road,
London W14 9PB, UK

www.blake.co.uk

First published in paperback in 2008

ISBN: 978-1-84454-511-7

A catalo⸀⸀⸀⸀⸀⸀⸀⸀⸀⸀⸀⸀⸀⸀⸀ ⸀e Bri⸀⸀⸀ Library.

Printed in Great Britain by CPI Bookmarque, Croydon CR0 4TD

1 3 5 7 9 10 8 6 4 2

Papers used by John Blake Publishing are natural, recyclable
products made from wood grown in sustainable forests.
The manufacturing processes conform to the environmental
regulations of the country of origin.

Every effort has been made to contact relevant copyright holders.
Any omission is inadvertent; we would be grateful if the appropriate
people could contact us.

To Jorge

Human beings are all members of one body.
They are created from the same essence.
When one member is in pain,
The others cannot rest.
If you do not care about the pain of others,
You do not deserve to be called a human being.
*Thirteenth-century Persian poet Saadi Shirazi*


Courage is fire, and bullying is smoke.
*Benjamin Disraeli*

BULLY

N.

A BLUSTERING BROWBEATING PERSON, ESPECIALLY ONE
HABITUALLY CRUEL TO OTHERS WHO ARE WEAKER

(MERRIAM-WEBSTER DICTIONARY)

# ACKNOWLEDGEMENTS

I'd like to thank the following people:
Jorge Lopez for being so supportive.
Wensley Clarkson for giving me the
opportunity to write this book.

# Contents

Prologue xiii

1: Mollie-Anna White, 12 1

2: Helen Green, 37 13

3: Sarah Costello, 18 31

4: Sandy Holt, 47 41

5: Becky Smith, 18 51

6: Sebastian Sharp, 31 63

7: Caroline Stillman, 14 73

8: Sophie Parks, 19 85

9: Kirsty Perkins, 14 97

10: Michael Shanley, 47 109

11: Abbi Morrall, 15 121

12: Mhairi Walker, 18 133

13: Amy Evans, 16                             145

14: Jacqui Gill, 45                           155

15: Georgia Foster, 41                        161

16: Maria Dixon, 40                           173

17: Abigail Worth, 18                         179

18: Oli Watts, 23                             189

19: Graham Mallaghan, 37                      201

20: Jenny Souter, 22                          213

Epilogue                                      223

Appendix A: Bullying Facts and Tips           231

Appendix B: Resources and Helplines           237

# Prologue

**A**ppearances can be deceptive. That child playing in the playground you pass on your way to work, that office worker in his neat suit, and even the man who delivers your post could be the victims of bullies. You would never know because more than half of victims of bullying never speak out about their ordeal through fear.

I have interviewed countless people during the course of this book. But it has been the victims themselves who have really provided me with the ability to explore the tragic effects that result from bullying.

As bullying reaches epidemic proportions in our schools and our neighbourhoods, it has become the single most important social issue today. It goes on in every country in the world and can have disastrous effects on the victim, such as suicide and even murder.

There seems to be one characteristic all bullies have in common: a desire to hurt their victim.

However, in this book, I have spoken to many people from all races, genders and ages who have suffered years of abuse at the hands of bullies, but managed to turn their lives around and make them a success.

They have beaten their bullies.

The clear message is: victims do not need to suffer in silence.

There is no code of honour that prevents you from asking for help. Bullying is wrong, in any situation. But it is the way that bullying is dealt with that makes the difference between a miserable life and a tolerable one.

I have used only information that I believe to be entirely accurate and if I have erred in any way it is in good faith. The dramatic quality of the cases means that they often read like fiction. And, while some readers may discover discrepancies between my version of events and what has been reported previously, I have sought to let the vivid truth occupy the centre stage.

This is what makes these cases all the more shocking and moving.

Polly Clarkson
Note: Names of bullies in some of the following case studies have been changed where indicated.

# Mollie-Anna White,12

'**C**ome on Mollie!' Kerry White shouted up to her twelve-year-old daughter. 'You'll be late for school if you don't hurry up.'

Bounding down the stairs, Mollie-Anna could feel the butterflies circling around her stomach. It was her first day at secondary school in September 2005 and Mollie-Anna was petrified.

Going through the important transition between primary and secondary school is always tough on children. Mollie-Anna White was no different. She had the same fears as every little girl would on her first day at school.

Will the others like me? Will I make any friends?

As she sat down at the table to eat her breakfast, Kerry could not believe her eyes.

'Oh, Mollie!' she said. 'Your hair's a mess and you haven't even done up your shoelaces.'

That was typical of Mollie-Anna. She was always in her own world, daydreaming.

Kerry grabbed a hairbrush and began combing through her daughter's knotted blonde hair.

'Mummy,' Mollie-Anna whispered, between mouthfuls of cereal. 'Will the other girls like me?'

Kerry reassured her daughter that she had nothing to worry about and packed her off on the local school bus. As she skipped off down the driveway, Mollie-Anna's fears soon turned into excitement. But it was short-lived.

Within a few hours of her starting at the new school, some of the girls in Mollie-Anna's class took a dislike to her and excluded her from the clique they were forming.

At first, Mollie-Anna brushed this off. She thought this was a usual part of secondary school.

But within days, this exclusion developed into intimidation. It started with money being stolen by a girl called Kelly*.

A month later, the abuse had escalated. Mollie-Anna was now being subjected to daily verbal attacks and even threatening phone calls – all from this same girl called Kelly.

*The name of the bully in this account has been changed.

At this stage, Mollie was brave enough to confide in her mother Kerry about what was going on at school.

Kerry, being an active member of the parent–teacher association, decided not only to give her daughter her full support and advice but also to pay close attention to how the school dealt with Mollie's dangerous predicament. Immediately, she asked Mollie to explain what had been happening to her teacher.

Mollie did so, but no action was taken by the school. By January 2006, the bullying had become so bad that Mollie was excluded from all social activity at school. She felt completely alone and desperate, and Kerry could not understand why her daughter was being bullied. Mollie had turned from a bubbly twelve-year-old into a scared, quiet young girl.

Kerry then decided she needed to gather evidence and started to tape the abusive phone calls.

That night, Mollie-Anna's mobile phone rang.

It was Kelly.

Mollie-Anna picked it up.

'If you come to school tomorrow,' Kelly told her. 'We'll beat you up, you stupid cow.'

Kerry listened in on the phone call and was appalled. She realised there was a serious problem, but knew she would need more evidence to take to the police in order to present a strong case.

'Mum,' Mollie-Anna said to her mother one night. 'I've written a poem about those girls.'

As Mollie-Anna read it out, the situation really hit home.

Make her stop mummy
Make her go away
Please Miss Oats I don't want to go out to play.
Why is it me Miss?
What have I done?
I just want to play and walk the other way
She is following me Miss
She punches me to the ground
My nose is bleeding
There's no-one around.
My name she calls I fall against the wall
Calling me names I start to bawl
She has gone finally I am free
I run home and
MY MUMMY SAVES ME

'It cut through me like a knife,' Kerry explains.

Kerry knew she needed to take action and finally put a stop to what was happening to her daughter.

But, suddenly, the bullying took an unexpected and modern twist.

When Mollie-Anna was at home one evening surfing on the Internet, safe from the bullies at school, or so she thought, Kelly added her as a friend on MSN and began to abuse her verbally. Mollie-Anna was horrified to open up her Hotmail and find this girl's abusive messages.

Not only did she need to suffer this indignity at school but now it had also infected her life at home.

She told her mother immediately, who advised her to tell her teachers. Once again, Mollie explained to the teacher what was happening and who the perpetrators were, but the school took no action.

'It was just constant. A couple of times the school sent Mollie home because they feared for her safety,' Kerry explains. 'Yet, nothing was done about it.'

During one incident in the playground in March, Mollie-Anna was surrounded by a bunch of girls who were harassing and intimidating her.

Mollie-Anna hit out and shouted at the girls to leave her alone.

But immediately Mollie was reprimanded by a teacher for losing her temper. Again, the bullies were never even spoken to. Mollie-Anna was suspended from school for one day.

But she was still receiving the abuse.

That night, she received a phone call at home, which was recorded by Kerry.

'We're gonna kill you,' Kelly told her. 'You're gonna get it real bad tomorrow.'

Armed with this evidence, Kerry marched into the school the next day and demanded to speak with the head teacher.

She explained that Mollie-Anna was extremely sorry for hitting back at the bully and knows that it was the wrong thing to do, but that the school needed to take responsibility for the bullying that was going on and do something about it.

That never happened.

Mollie-Anna came back to school to an extremely hostile environment.

A few days later, the bullies, who included Kelly and a group of other girls from her year, chased Mollie-Anna into the toilets.

Mollie sought refuge in a cubicle with the door locked and called her mother from her mobile.

Kerry, upon hearing her daughter's loud screams and the threats at the end of the phone, called the school on her landline phone.

She was in a state of utter panic.

'I'll just transfer you,' the school's receptionist told Kerry calmly.

But Kerry went straight through to the head-master's voice mail.

Immediately she rang back and explained that her daughter was being attacked in the toilets.

'Please, don't put me through to a mailbox,' she pleaded.

Once again, she was transferred to his answer machine.

Kerry hung up.

She realised then that the school were completely unwilling to help.

Instead, she dialled 999.

'Please, someone help,' she told the police operator. 'My daughter's being beaten up at school!'

The police arrived at the school within minutes and rescued Mollie-Anna.

'Your daughter's in safe hands now,' the officer told Kerry, leading Mollie-Anna out of the cubicle.

They interviewed all the girls involved in the incident. But matters did not improve. Later that same week, another violent incident occurred where Mollie-Anna was physically attacked by a group of girls.

As she fled her bullies, she phoned her mother once more for help. Frustrated, Kerry called the police again. But the school still refused to accept that there was any bullying taking place.

Kerry resorted to the last thing she wanted to do and took Mollie-Anna out of school.

'I wasn't prepared to send her somewhere where her physical safety was no longer assured,' she explains.

Kerry spent the next few months trying to find a solution to the problem. She looked for other schools in the area, but there were no places available. The entire family were at their wits' end.

Although Mollie-Anna was out of school, the bullying continued – this time all on MSN. One particular evening Mollie-Anna was online. Kelly started to harass her, so Mollie-Anna went and showed her mother.

'You're such a loser,' the message read. 'You should just kill yourself.'

Kerry immediately asked Mollie to leave the room.

Normally Kerry would step in and block the girl's messages, but this time she decided to have a heart-to-heart with Kelly on the Net. She wanted to tackle the situation head-on.

Kerry went against most anti-bullying advice and sat down at the computer and spoke to the bully.

Kerry told the girl that she did not think her mother would want her to be a bully.

Immediately Kelly asked her what that meant.

'No parent wants their child to be a bully,' Kerry says.

Kelly then explained that she had not intended to bully Mollie-Anna.

'It's not because of Mollie,' Kelly admitted. 'It's because of what happens at home.'

Kelly went on to describe how her father would lose his temper and take his anger out on her.

'I realised they were both victims,' Kerry concluded.

Through the ensuing conversations, which went on over days, Kerry was able to explain to Kelly the effect of her actions.

Eventually, Kerry was even able to broker a renewed friendship between the two girls, which had seemed unbelievable only a few weeks previously.

Kerry now feels that frank exchange helped the girl see what she was doing was wrong. Kelly even took it upon herself to write a letter of apology to Mollie-Anna.

Finally, after nine months, Mollie-Anna's misery had come to an end. But the problem with the school remained.

Although Kerry was able to solve the bullying problem, her confidence in the school's ability to do this was shattered.

She also desperately needed to get her daughter back into the education system.

She decided to get involved with the anti-bullying charity BeatBullying to try to get her cause publicised. She also hoped to bring BeatBullying into the school to run workshops to solve the bullying problem. As a result, she was able to involve key figures from the charity, which finally led the local MP to step in on her behalf to help get Mollie-Anna back to school.

In September 2006, more than a hundred pupils from Mollie-Anna's school wrote a petition to get Mollie-Anna back.

Kerry sent Mollie-Anna back to school just days later.

Now Kerry believes that teaching social skills could have prevented the attacks.

'I feel that Mollie's bully is a victim as well, because you don't give birth to a bully,' she says. 'These children don't have any social skills towards one another. These youngsters are so negative in their outlook. They need to be taught life skills.'

Kerry feels the lesson is that parents and teachers must not sweep bullying under the carpet.

'I really think that if your child is being bullied you've got to step up and shout until you're heard,' she says.

She believes so many children are forced to call the charity ChildLine because they cannot speak to their parents.

'I think the most positive thing to do is to sit around the table and have set mealtimes. Have a set time each day when there are no mobiles and no computers on,' she adds.

As a result of what happened to Mollie-Anna White, from September 2006, every eleven-year-old in the Tyneside area had to be put through a special 'anti-depression' programme. This included lessons in building up self-esteem, special sessions on helping children to cope with warring parents, and even relaxation and negotiation techniques.

At the same time, child welfare experts warned that schools focus all their attention on disruptive children, because of the national obsession with antisocial behaviour, and neglect the needs of those pupils who may not be disruptive but are still struggling to cope with emotional issues.

For Mollie-Anna White at least, the future's now bright.

# 2

# Helen Green, 37

**W**alking through the gleaming portals of Deutsche Bank in the City of London, brunette Helen Green adjusted her tight black pencil skirt and took a deep breath. It was October 1997 on her first day as company secretary and she was ridden with nerves.

She was proud of herself – she had got there without privilege or even support.

'All I wanted to be from the age of nineteen was a company secretary,' she says.

A company secretary manages the processes that ensure the organisation complies with company legislation and regulation and keeps board members informed of their legal responsibilities.

But the City is a hyper version of other offices. The hours are long and the place throbs with testosterone. And Frankfurt-based Deutsche Bank is the world's third-biggest investment bank.

Having escaped her abusive adoptive father at the age of sixteen, Helen had moved into a bedsit, worked and put herself through university to get a degree over a number of years. Finally, at the age of twenty-seven, she had embarked on a business career. Reaching the Square Mile, for her, was the pinnacle of her life.

But, just six weeks after starting at Deutsche Bank, Helen realised her dream job was not as perfect as she had imagined. One day, four of her female colleagues asked her for lunch. Helen was so overwhelmed by her new workload that she refused.

'It seemed rude. But I was attending meetings and wasn't in the department much,' she says. 'I was focusing on work.'

But that insignificant rejection unleashed a campaign of abuse. From the outside, the gang of women picking on Helen sounded petty: silent staring, laughter intended to intimidate or unnerve her, crude comments and the removal of papers from her desk.

But the bullying was systematic.

'I'm not some little wallflower,' Helen insists. 'I

played hockey to county level; I won a golf competition; I skydived with people from the army. I'm used to the odd lewd comment. I didn't crumble at the first push.'

Instead of approaching her individually, they 'mobbed' her. Mobbing, or ganging up on a victim, was a behaviour first observed in female birds. It is how they try to protect their nests from predators.

Helen Green's tormentors used strength in numbers. A colleague blew raspberries as Helen walked across the room. 'What's that stink in here?' she also shouted before gesturing towards Helen.

Her name was also removed from the firm's global intranet directory and from departmental circulation lists.

'One of the women made it very clear that she wasn't even going to acknowledge me when she walked past me. Normal etiquettes, corridor etiquettes when you smile at someone – she would just focus her eye contact into the distance to the point where I had to talk to her about it,' she says.

Helen said that it got to the stage where she would just sit at her desk and cry silently.

'I felt that this was my career. It was my third job as company secretary and the reason I chose Deutsche Bank over other companies is because you could have very long-term prospects. I'm talking of a life career. It's such a large organisation and you can go as high as you want,' she says.

When she first complained in March 1998, she was determined to make the job work and did not want to be seen as a troublemaker.

'I was very upset with the whole situation. It wasn't something I wanted to pursue. I just wanted to keep my head down, get on with my job and be appreciated for the quality of the work I was doing,' she says.

But Personnel's response was that the best way of dealing with it was to talk to the women. Other colleagues also told her not to worry about the behaviour.

There was another factor that may explain some of the animosity of her colleagues. After a few months in her new job Helen began a relationship with the head of the company secretariat department, Richard Elliston, her ultimate boss, who was in charge of the division, rather than the man she reported to every day.

Elliston was nearly twice her age and married, but separated from his wife. It all began when Elliston invited Helen to lunch and the opera. Soon they had embarked on a full-blown affair, openly outside office hours and discreetly around the water cooler. Clearly it was an intense relationship.

But he did not help her stamp out the bullying.

The affair lasted five years before Helen finished the relationship in 2002.

But she insists their affair had no impact on the bullying and was not the reason for her colleagues' cattiness.

'No. My relationship had no bearing on the bullying,' she says.

Elliston later admitted in court that he should have done more.

Helen also claimed that one of the gang's nastier attacks was to ask her what it was like to perform a sexual act on a man without a foreskin – Helen is Jewish.

But the bullying wasn't limited to the women in the office: Helen was also harassed by male managers who drove her to a further nervous breakdown.

Indeed, attempts to steal her job seem to have affected her the most. 'The women are incidental, really. It is not the name calling that did me: it was targeting my career – to some at Deutsche it was a sport.'

By December 1999, office life grew so bad that Helen felt too scared to use the toilet as the gang stared at her 'threateningly'.

'I followed the manual. I made the people concerned aware that I was unhappy,' she says.

But the only time Helen's management reacted was when they openly studied a document revealing the salary of a proposed secretary.

While those who complained of bullying were sent on assertiveness training, the rest were dispatched to a harassment-awareness course.

After returning from a holiday in Egypt in 2000, Helen Green attempted to return to work but found that she was simply unable to make herself walk through the main door of her employer's offices.

She eventually convinced herself to go back. But the final step of her unhappy Deutsche career came when she discovered an email between two senior managers seemingly hinting that they needed to axe her. This sent her into another decline.

She was then referred to a doctor, and, the following day, was admitted to hospital, where a major depressive disorder was diagnosed. Her condition was such that she was put on suicide watch for the first couple of days and remained an inpatient until Christmas Eve 2000.

She then lived in a 'halfway house' attached to the hospital until the end of January 2001. In March 2001, she returned to work, initially part-time. In October 2001, she suffered a relapse of the psychiatric illness and at the end of the month stopped work and did not return. Her employment was ended by Deutsche Bank in September 2003.

For two years she was off work – on full pay. It sounds as if the bank was generous in keeping her on the payroll through such a long period of inactivity.

But Helen disagrees. 'They kept asking when I was returning to work. But I was so ill by this stage with side effects of medication. For five days I didn't so much as draw the curtains.'

Seven days later she sued the bank by filing proceedings in the High Court in London. The case was bought under English law and was in part based on the Protection from Harassment Act 1997 (UK). This legislation, under which Helen Green won her case, was drawn up to prevent stalkers from making victims' lives a misery.

Before this Act, workplace bullying victims would have gone to an employment tribunal for compensation. This one was brought in the High Court of Justice in London in July 2006.

Helen Green also argued her case based on the law of negligence and breaches of her contract of employment.

It was one of a number of significant cases in Britain dealing with bullying and consequential psychiatric disorder.

Helen told the judge that the banter was not

playful but malicious and vicious. She said she suffered psychiatric injury because of 'the offensive, abusive, intimidating bullying, and the humiliating, patronising, infantile, and insulting words and behaviour of the four women'.

She was left crying silently at her desk and eventually suffered a nervous breakdown.

Her former personal assistant, Clare McCall, told the court of the level of noise and bullying in the office.

'I have never come across anything like it before or since,' she said. 'When the women realised they could get away with treating her as they pleased, they went for the kill.'

Justice Owen accepted Helen Green's evidence that, before a male member of staff had started bullying her, he had told her he had met two of the bullies on the staircase.

He then heard one say to the other, 'God, did you see her face? We nearly got her crying this time.' And the other one replied, 'Good – who does she think she is?'

'Bullying in all its forms, if tolerated by employers, has a corrosive effect, causes great suffering and wastes valuable human resources,' interrupted Tony Morton-Hooper, Helen Green's solicitor. 'It also makes a mockery of senior management's fine words about respecting and understanding others.'

Cross-examining, Geoffrey Brown suggested to Helen that the women were 'just ordinary decent people'.

'In my experience of their behaviour, no,' Helen replied. 'I think I was just the next person in the firing line.'

Brown also suggested that Helen Green was not always pleasant to them.

'I always tried my best under very difficult circumstances,' she responded.

Brown said that the women would say hello to Helen, but she would acknowledge them only when it suited her.

'That just isn't true. When you are being bullied, you can't do anything right. For them to say I didn't smile at them... they had me in tears,' she said.

'Everyone knew about the bullying, the managers and Human Resources. Some of it was quite horrific,' Heather Cook, who also worked for Deutsche Bank, told Justice Owen. Heather Cook said she took two months' sick leave in the late nineties after being subjected to bullying by the same group of women.

But she said the intimidation campaign eventually 'lessened' on her as her tormentors 'started on Helen'.

'I knew what Helen was going through because I was going through it too. I saw Helen was quite distressed,' she said.

Clare McCall, then told the court, 'It was intimidation. It was... childish behaviour'.

She also said that Helen Green was deliberately excluded for no reason by others, who engaged in 'schoolyard tactics'.

Deutsche Bank immediately denied that Helen Green was bullied or harassed or subjected to improper or unreasonable conduct. It claimed that she would not have continued with the firm beyond September 2003 in any case because of growing dissatisfaction with her performance and attitude.

Cross-examining, Geoffrey Brown contested her claim that Deutsche Bank was well aware that she had a pre-existing vulnerability because of her childhood. But in her written evidence, Helen was adamant that the bank knew about her condition.

'The cause of my breakdown, however, was the treatment which I was subjected to while employed by the defendant,' she said.

But Brown suggested that Helen was not giving a 'fair picture' of what went on. She did agree, however, that she had never told Personnel, when she made her complaints, that she was having an ongoing relationship with the department head Richard Elliston.

'No, it was a separate matter. I wasn't complaining about Richard: I was complaining about the bullies,' she said.

She rejected Geoffrey Brown's claim that her relationship with Elliston was foundering by November 2000, when she was admitted to hospital, and that afterwards she started instigating complaints about him.

Justice Owen commented that bullying in that department was a longstanding problem to which other employees had fallen victim.

He described the bank's management as 'weak and ineffectual' and said the managers 'collectively closed their eyes to what was going on, no doubt in the hope that the problem would go away'.

Helen satisfied the judge that the bullying was not isolated but cultural. She recalled how a colleague was under so much stress during pregnancy that she contracted pneumonia and miscarried, while her bosses 'closed their eyes'.

Under UK occupational-health-and-safety law, employers have a legal duty to identify, assess and control all health-and-safety hazards in the workplace.

To succeed in stress-at-work claims, employees

must prove that bosses knew or ought to have known that their workplace treatment could cause a psychiatric illness.

Helen Green succeeded on this count and also in an additional argument that the bullying amounted to harassment under the Protection from Harassment Act.

The court found that she had been the victim of 'a deliberate and concerted campaign of bullying'.

Justice Owen ruled that Deutsche Bank Group Services was responsible for causing her two nervous breakdowns and a major depressive disorder as a result of its 'relentless campaign of mean and spiteful behaviour designed to cause her distress'.

It was a warning shot to companies to take bullying seriously.

Owen also decided that the 'wholly abnormal stress' she suffered from the bullying at work, and not her difficult childhood, was to blame for the mental illness she suffered.

However, in court the bank suggested that if she had disclosed the full extent of her past troubles it might have had pause for thought.

The story of Helen's childhood is a complicated one. She was a product of an affair between her Jewish Orthodox mother and her Italian father. The Jewish community of Leeds was scandalised. The family forced Helen Green's mother to send her to a Manchester children's home.

'Her family would not let me in the house,' says Helen, tears welling in her brown eyes.

So, aged two, she was given up for adoption to another Jewish family in Lincolnshire.

Her adoptive father, Edward Green (now dead), was a wealthy accountant who drove a Rolls-Royce. He was well known as charming and generous – apparently, the perfect family man.

Six months after fostering the little girl, the couple, who already had two adopted sons, officially adopted Helen. Then, when she was six, the family moved to a seven-bedroom, stone manor house, complete with stables.

To the outside world at least, it must have seemed as if they had an idyllic family life. However, that is not how Helen recalls it.

Helen believes the sexual abuse began almost as soon as she was adopted.

'I can remember him coming to my bedroom regularly, more than once a week, in the dead of night,' she says. 'He'd always be wearing pyjamas. I felt as if I had to be as still as possible so as not to give him any idea that I was awake.

'He was over six foot tall and fifteen stone. A big man. I'm only five foot three now.

'His weight on the mattress made me slide towards him, even though I would try to keep myself away. He would try to make me participate. "You can't pretend you're asleep," he would say.

'He would ask me if I was enjoying myself. He'd say to me "Does it tickle?" as if he were doing something I liked. I was so young and afraid that I agreed to do anything he said.'

The abuse continued until she was eleven. She says she endured two more incidents in the following two years. But not once did Helen tell a soul about what was happening.

'Nobody talked about sexual abuse back then,' she explains.

This harrowing ordeal changed Helen, as it would any child.

She claimed to have suffered insomnia, phobias and depression, which have continued to this day.

In 1991, Helen took Edward Green to the civil court for what she claimed were eleven years of frequent and distressing childhood sexual abuse that left her psychologically scarred.

A civil action, she was advised, was her best chance of getting justice against her father.

Edward Green admitted sexual abuse and, after a two-day hearing, the judge found against him. He was ordered to pay his daughter £17,000 in damages.

'I wanted justice. I needed to convince myself it was not my fault – and, above all, to give hope to silent victims. I hope my action will give them the courage to come forward and speak out. I'm not happy about anything, but I am glad my father has got to pay,' Helen said at the time of the court case.

He was later cautioned and put on the sex offenders' register.

The anguish drove Helen to a breakdown and she has been estranged from the rest of her adoptive family ever since.

'That was why I was such a reluctant litigant this time,' she says.

'I'd been through the legal process. I understood the tactics and trauma.' Deutsche Bank looked into Helen's family background.

Indirectly, its probing had a bittersweet ending – it led Helen Green to trace her real family for the first time.

I didn't even know the full circumstances of my adoption. But last year I contacted social services and discovered my natural mother had passed away two years ago; I just missed her,' she says.

However, amid such bleakness Helen Green found hope – she finally met her biological brother in 2005.

'He's lovely,' she beamed. 'He was able to tell me

so much. I feel I could write a book about my family.'

In August 2006, Helen Green was awarded £817,317. This included £35,000 for pain and suffering, £25,000 in respect of disadvantage in the labour market, £128,000 for past lost earnings and about £640,000 for future lost earnings. The bank also had to pay her legal costs.

We are told this and other legal decisions give employers a clear mandate to draw up a bullying policy and make staff aware of the unacceptability of workplace bullying.

Deutsche Bank denied wrongdoing and said it paid for stress counselling and other therapy for Helen while she was employed.

Outside court, Helen said she was 'delighted' with the decision, saying it marked the end of a 'long and painful battle'.

'In fighting my case, I have become more aware of what a big problem bullying is in the City,' she said. 'My case was not an isolated one.'

Helen Green warned that bullying was rife in the City of London.

'Now all City businesses will have to do more than pay lip service to this hidden menace,' she said.

She's just glad to be out of that 'department of hell'.

'Deutsche has taken nine years of my life. This money has to last me a long time. It's in return for destroying my career. The case has broken my heart.'

Now Helen wants to devote time to protecting others like herself.

It had destroyed her dreams of having a successful career with the bank, but now she wants to become a lecturer in organisational behaviour. This decision was motivated by her experiences at Deutsche Bank.

'I am going into an academic career so that I can learn about this, look at the issues... and hopefully find ways of dealing with them.'

'I am thirty-six with no career; it'll be hard,' she says.

Before her ordeal, Helen Green was earning £65,000 a year. In the two years after she left the bank, she had been fighting her case and been living in London's East End on social security.

'I've fallen a long way behind with so much of my life,' she says with regard to marriage and children. 'Anyone who has ever been bullied at work will know that it takes over your whole life, can change your personality, lowers self-esteem, ends relationships – and sometimes life itself,' she adds.

Helen is just glad that she fought for justice against a multi-billion dollar corporation – and won.

# 3

# Sarah Costello, 18

Sarah Costello sat quietly at her wooden desk, opened up her rucksack and reached for her notepad. It was June 2000.

The sun was shining brightly and there was not a single cloud outside. It was a perfect summer day for the residents of Doncaster.

With picturesque villages, historic market and unspoiled countryside, this bustling town in South Yorkshire is a very popular tourist attraction for the rest of the country, and it is even more beautiful in the summer time.

As Sarah listened intently to her teacher explaining the rules of algebra, she felt someone poke her in the back. She jolted and turned around.

'Hey!' she said to fellow pupil Jane.* 'What you doing?'

But that didn't deter Jane. It just provoked her even more.

'Hey, Tracey,' Jane said to her friend sitting next to her. 'Cry Baby's got a problem with my ruler. Let's poke her again!'

Both girls then started to stick their rulers into Sarah's back.

'Leave me alone,' she pleaded. 'What's your problem?'

But the girls just kept nudging her in the back. Sarah moved her desk forward, hoping that would deter them. But it just provoked the girls even more and they moved their seats forward too. Eventually, after about ten minutes, the girls got bored.

There was nothing unusual about this scene – it was just a typical day for Sarah.

The bullying started in Year Seven. A few girls in her class started to call her ugly and told her she needed to lose weight. But it quickly got worse. Within a few weeks, Sarah was regularly being verbally attacked by these girls. Every day became like a nightmare for her.

'I think it started because I'm so tall and they

*Names of bullies in this account have been changed.

must have felt I stood out and was an easy target for abuse,' she says.

But the situation was about to get a whole lot worse. One of her close friends began bullying Sarah. At one point, she burned Sarah with a soldering iron in the technology class. She claimed it had been an accident.

Sarah felt betrayed and lonely.

Day after day, Sarah dreaded going to school. In the end, she moved tutor groups and the bullying stopped. But this did not last long. In fact, it was about to get worse. The afternoons were particularly bad when Sarah had to catch the bus home.

'I dreaded it when my mum was working late,' she says. 'I didn't want to be alone in my house.'

People she didn't even know would shout things in her ear and throw newspapers at her. One time, it got so bad that Sarah had to get off the bus before it even left the school drive.

'I remember that day as clear as anything. I was looking at strangers on the bus thinking, "Please, help me, make them stop,"' she says.

Every time her bullies caught her eye, they'd look away.

'It got to the stage I stopped taking the newspaper off me, I stopped doing anything, I just sat in a ball and let them do what they wanted to. They'd be getting off the bus soon anyway,' she says.

Another time, after a particularly vicious attack by another girl, Sarah started to cry uncontrollably in the school playground.

'I was crying so hard I couldn't even stand up and I'd never cried at school before,' she says.

More bullying started up after that. Sarah's vulnerability only fuelled the fire. People would come up behind her and pretend to cry in her ear.

Once, when she was walking down the corridor, two girls slapped Sarah just to see how she would react, whether she would hit them back, leave it or cry. They would knock her bag off her back then pretend to cry.

Sarah was miserable. She tried to block out the voices, but it was impossible.

'The most vivid memory I had was when I was standing outside with my best mate, and these girls came up to me who had bullied me in the past. They were pulling my hair, asking why I straightened it. They were pulling it hard, and I wanted to die right there and then,' says Sarah.

Another time, Sarah was walking down the school drive with one of her friends. They were talking when another girl from their class approached them and shoved them deliberately.

Sarah stood still. 'Don't react,' she whispered to her friend.

'I'll knock you out if you don't shut your gob,' the girl shouted at Sarah, standing with a gang of other girls.

As Sarah and her friend tried to walk away from the girl, the gang followed them. At one point, Sarah stopped, pretending to get something out of her bag, but the group of girls stood and waited for them.

Sarah and her friend then tried to cross to the other side of the road. But the ringleader stood in the middle of the road and said she was going to follow them whichever way they went.

Fortunately for Sarah, their head of year passed by to catch the bus and the gang of girls stopped shouting abuse at them. But, as soon as he had disappeared, they started up again. They were shouting all sorts of abuse.

Thankfully, the girls had another lucky escape. Sarah's dad was at the bottom of the drive in the car, so they got in and drove off.

Sarah did not mention the day's events to her father. She dreaded her parents finding out. She felt so much shame for being bullied. She was terrified that people would think it was her fault, that she was the one with a problem.

Despite everything being so bad, Sarah never missed a day of school. She went every single day, unless she was genuinely ill. But she spent most lunchtimes in the library.

'I'm really sick of spending break alone,' Sarah said to her mum, Jean, one day.

She hoped her mum would understand.

'You just need to make more friends,' she told Sarah.

At this point, Jean had no idea that her daughter was being physically and verbally abused at school. How could Sarah explain to her mother that she wanted to sit on her own rather than with her bullies?

Sarah bottled everything up and told no one about what was happening. She was so scared people might think she deserved it because she was too vulnerable to stand up to her bullies. In fact, for years, Sarah believed it was her fault.

It was only later that she realised that no one deserves to be bullied, or asks to be bullied.

Then in September 2004 Sarah's grandmother died. It was a big blow to Sarah, since her gran was really close to her.

By now, the bullying had calmed down. But Sara would remember things from her days of being bullied and start to feel angry. She started self-harming as a way of coping.

'I overdosed on my hay-fever medication several times – not with the intention of suicide, but I saw it as another way of hurting myself,' she says.

It was painful, but it was a release from her problems. Everything Sarah had valued in her life had begun to slip away.

'My body was there but my mind wasn't, my mind was elsewhere,' she says.

She would force herself to get up and go to school every day but it was a struggle.

Her other outlet was to write in her diary. It helped Sarah work through her feelings of hurt, fear and anger. She would see visions of her bullies taunting her. It was terrifying for her but she knew it was important.

Sarah, to this day, will not release what she wrote in her diary entries.

'The entries are too disturbing,' she says.

At the beginning of 2005, Sarah's mother spotted her daughter's diary while she was cleaning her room one day. Curiosity got the better of her. She opened it up and read page after page. It was then that she realised her daughter was in desperate need of help.

Jean told the school and ordered Sarah's headmaster to take action. But, despite offering Sarah counselling and assuring her they would deal with her bullies appropriately, Sarah's scars were still raw.

She started counselling at a nearby hospital once a week. Sarah felt an emotional load being lifted off her. But, by the second week, Sarah's bullies started up again.

As a result, Sarah became too scared to continue her counselling for fear of her bullies finding out.

Instead, she searched the Internet for websites about bullying. She came across sites such as http://www.beatingthebullies.org. Finding out more about what bullying meant and what other people were going through made her feel less isolated.

As she scrolled through all the advice, what Sarah found online helped her so much. As a result, she decided to set up her own website against bullying.

In 2004, she followed a step-by-step tutorial on how to make a website and wrote the content herself. She called it Stop Bullying Now [now called Stamp Out Bullying].

It was easier than she thought and took Sarah only a few days to get it started. The website was meant to help victims of bullying or people who have been bullied in the past.

'No one deserves to be bullied, and we are here to encourage victims to speak out,' Sarah now says. 'I felt proud that other people might read my advice, and, although I found it quite upsetting to write about what I was going through, it made me feel better that my experiences might help someone else.'

Now the site has had more than two thousand hits.

As well as to prevent other people suffering from bullying at school, setting up the website has changed Sarah's life and given her confidence. She was nominated for the Spirit of Doncaster Young Person's Award for setting it up. She also finished her counselling sessions at the end of 2005.

'In a way, I could say I'm glad about what happened. It's true. What doesn't kill you makes you stronger. Believe me, if you have faith in yourself, you can get through anything. You just need to hold your head up high and get through it,' she says.

'Tell someone, because that's the mistake I made, and a lot of people, understandably, do make it. If you let your bully get away with it, there's going to be more victims that feel like you. You're not alone, don't feel ashamed, tell someone.

'There have got to be more survivors in this world, and I'm proud to say I'm a survivor!' she says. 'I know there are alternatives to hurting myself. I still have bad days when I don't particularly want to get up and face the world but I'm not going to let a bunch of losers ruin everything I pieced back together,' she says.

Jean is very proud of the work her daughter is doing to help others.

'I'm at college now in another town, and I love it. I have amazing friends who love me,' she says.

Sarah's story goes to show that anyone can achieve their dream.

You can visit Sarah's website at http://stampoutbullying.tripod.com.

Note: Sarah's mother Jean died in 2006.

# 4

# Sandy Holt, 47

As Sandy Holt pounded the punchbag with his thick red gloves at his boxing club in Bolton, a town in northern England, an image from his childhood flashed through his mind.

'You're gonna get it good today, Gingernut!' an older boy from his school shouted at him.

Sandy was used to the name-calling: he had been terrorised by a gang of six older boys, nicknamed 'the Boys', for years. They mostly targeted the younger pupils at Hayward School in Great Lever, just outside Bolton.

But Sandy was pinpointed in particular because of his short stature, red hair and freckles.

'For some reason, they always wanted to use me

as a punchbag,' he says. 'They were a frightening pack and, like big, strong types do, they picked on the weaker, young ones.'

It all started three years before, when Sandy was twelve. He was walking home from school one day when the boys approached him.

'Oi!' they sniggered, shoving Sandy. 'Short, ginger and ugly. You really lucked out.'

Sandy was helpless. He knew he could not fight back against six boys. Instead, he stood defenceless as each boy took it in turns to punch Sandy with all his force.

As Sandy limped home that evening, covered in cuts and bruises, he knew his life would never be the same again. From then on, he was subjected to relentless bullying by the Boys.

'They used to nick the kids' dinner money, but they really delighted in beating me up,' he recalls.

On one occasion, they dragged Sandy to the school toilets and punched and kicked him until he was knocked unconscious. Sandy's injuries were so bad that day that he ended up in hospital with internal bleeding.

After that, Sandy decided to tell his teachers. But the Boys found out and took revenge. On his way home the next day, Sandy was beaten up even more ferociously than usual.

'Schools didn't deal with bullying like they do today,' says Sandy.

But he never missed a day's schooling because of it. He was always determined not to let his bullies ruin his life.

However, at the age of fifteen, on the day before his final day of secondary school, Sandy found out what the gang intended for him.

'They were going to tie me to a chair and throw me in the swimming pool,' he says. 'And I knew they were capable of doing this.'

Sandy decided not to attend class that day.

'But that was the only time, because education was important to me,' he adds.

The day after Sandy left school, he searched the Internet for self-defence classes.

'I wanted to be able to fight back,' he says.

Because he measured only five foot two inches, Sandy could not rely on physical strength alone and had to find an alternative route.

'I was one of the Bruce Lee generation boom. Seeing Bruce Lee doing his stuff on the big screen set my imagination running riot,' he says.

Watching Bruce Lee led him to believe that martial arts could be his way out from the hell at school. As he scrolled through the list of websites related to Bruce Lee, he came across one about karate.

'Fight back!' it read, before describing all the different forms of martial arts available in the UK.

Without hesitation, Sandy decided to enrol on his nearest karate course.

'It was a way to increase my confidence and self-esteem,' he says.

In early 1974, Sandy began his first karate training session. He stuck at this for three years and trained at least four times a week.

'I never missed a class,' he says.

Gradually, Sandy became proficient in karate.

Then, in 1977, he read an advert in the local newspaper about a new class opening up in Bolton.

'Learn the awesome kicks of Muay Thai,' it read.

Sandy was intrigued. The following week, he went along to the training centre to take a look.

That day changed his life.

Sandy sat there almost numb with disbelief as he saw the trainer, Master Sken, go through his repertoire of techniques. He had seen a lot of martial arts over the previous three years – but nothing compared to this.

'Master Sken was soaring up into the air and hitting suspended kickbags with elbows, knees and feet with the same amount of power a boxer hits a punchbag,' he says.

That moment influenced Sandy's life for ever.

With the demo over, he joined on the spot.

A week later, he was dressed in his Muay Thai clothing, a karate suit and brown belt, not knowing what to expect.

For a time, Sandy continued to train in karate due to loyalty. But eventually, about four months down the line, he declined his karate black belt and started training solely in Muay Thai, which is Thai kickboxing. He trained almost every day of the week.

'I'm an extremist by nature,' he says. 'This new training occupied almost every waking moment of my life.'

About three years after starting Muay Thai, Sandy had his first amateur Thai-boxing fight. He won. He went on to fight for his first British title in 1987 held under the old British Thai Boxing Council, which at the time was the governing body for Thai boxing in Great Britain.

He won the title.

His second British title was later that year at the All Styles contest.

With two titles under his belt, it was a far cry from the days when Sandy was bullied.

'I have never been bullied since. And I would never let anyone I know be bullied,' he says. 'Through the martial training I have done I have proved that a smaller man can defeat a larger man.'

In 1987, exactly a decade after he first started training, Sandy hung up his gloves. He retired from the ring, with two British Titles and a European Title behind him.

'A decade in the ring is more than most people achieve,' he says.

Once Sandy stopped fighting, he concentrated more on teaching instructors the art of Muay Thai. His set up his club, the Bolton Thai-Boxing Club, and it rapidly expanded.

It was one of the first Thai kickboxing schools in the country.

'The transition from fighter to trainer was not as tough as I thought it would be,' he says.

All his hard work paid off.

'It always amazed me how much dedication students placed on training with me,' he says.

One of his students travelled a 500-mile round trip every week to train with Sandy. This boy is now the owner of one of the biggest Thai-boxing organisations in Scotland.

Sandy was presented with his Red and Silver Monkon in 2006, a ceremonial headband, for his twenty years' service to Muay Thai, by Master Sken.

It was an award from Master to student in recognition of loyalty.

It is also the highest award a student can receive from his Master – before becoming a Gold, which is the mark of the Master.

And it was also the first ever award Master Sken had given to any of his pupils.

But Sandy's life could have gone in a very different direction.

'I feel I could have gone the suicide route,' he says. 'Luckily I turned a negative into a positive and channelled all the frustrations of being beaten up into training.'

That is Sandy's drive. Even now, Sandy trains for hours and does more than a thousand press-ups a day.

'Revenge is a very pertinent point on one's mind when you're being bullied,' he says.

As for having his revenge over the Boys, Sandy has managed that – without laying a hand on them.

'I've met three of them individually, and they were all scared of me,' he says. 'In fact, one of them grovelled in front of me and begged me not to hit him. That, and my own successes, have proved the best revenge of all.'

Sandy is now involved in a campaign in the United Kingdom called Bully Busters, which involves going into schools and teaching children how to stand up to bullies.

'It's part psychological and part physical training,' he says.

The success of his concept is now being studied to see if it can be adopted nationwide.

Sandy even went back to his old school in a bid to inspire young people. And the youngsters ended up taking part in filming for a TV documentary, The Size of the Man, which was screened on Five in early 2007. It followed people who have overcome adversity in their life due to their size and gone on to achieve great things.

Sandy picked his old school to appear in the short film.

A week-long series of events was organised to mark the anti-bullying week, including a poster competition and the writing of a short piece on what it would be like to be bullied. Children also took part in role-play activities. The week ended with a talk by Sandy, who spoke about his experiences of being bullied as a child. The event, sponsored by local firms, was organised by parents and staff.

'We want other schools to learn from Hayward School's work in raising awareness of bullying,' said a parent, Julie Davies, who helped organise the event. 'The school does not have a problem with bullying but it is important to raise the issue.'

The assistant headteacher, Sandi Reid, said, 'He held an assembly to urge children to make the most of all their experiences, even negative ones, and turn them around into something positive. Sandy told the pupils he really enjoyed school and never missed a day. But he spoke about how a small number of pupils made his life at school difficult and how, as a result of that, he turned to Thai boxing.'

Then, in April 2007, representatives of the annual reference book *Guinness World Records* attended a record attempt in Bolton for the most press-ups performed in an hour. The event was to recognise all the men and women who have contributed to Bolton's Spirit of Sport, which is a piece of public art dedicated to Bolton's sporting community. Standing at approximately 30 metres (100 feet) tall, the sculpture is constructed of stainless steel and has a golden appearance with its surface 'tiled' with nine hundred etched images of sporting heroes.

Sandy Holt, the record challenger, was one of them.

The atmosphere was unbelievably charged as it appeared that most of Bolton had turned up to support the attempt. They cheered almost continuously for the whole hour as Sandy fought to complete more and more press-ups.

Unfortunately, his total at the end of the hour fell short of a new record as he completed 2,952 press-ups against the present record of 3,416.

One of the most striking aspects about Sandy, however, was how he appeared completely calm and relaxed immediately after he had finished the hour's extreme exertion.

Though his mind-over-matter approach did not quite get him the record this time, Sandy is not a man to be beaten.

'I'm not an angry person,' he insists. 'But I take my aggression out in the gym, and anyone will tell you that, outside it, I'm a happy person!'

For now, Sandy wants to carry on educating young people about the effects of bullying.

'I've always campaigned against bullying because I know how it feels,' he said. 'The most important thing is to tell somebody what is happening to you – either a teacher or your parents – and get help. Thai boxing is a great way to build up your self-esteem and learn how to protect yourself.

'Being bullied really hurt. But it made me focus and I now I visit schools to try to get the anti-bullying message across,' he adds.

# 5

# Becky Smith, 18

As Becky Smith walked down the street on a Monday evening in May 2005, she smiled.

She had just left her best friend Shana's house and the sun was shining. She looked at her watch and realised it was 7.15 p.m.

I'd better head home, she thought. Her mother, Georgina Smith, would be wondering where she was.

Just as she set off, she spotted a friend called Sam from Plant Hill High School in Blackley, Manchester, walking towards her.

'Hi, Becky!' he said. 'How's it going?'

They started chatting about their GCSEs, which they were taking soon, and sat down on some steps further along the street.

## BEATING THE BULLIES

'We'd better pass them or we'll be stuck at school all our lives!' Sam teased. Becky giggled. She was really looking forward to going to her local college to study drama – but she had to pass her exams first.

What happened next came out of the blue.

Out of nowhere Becky felt a really hard kick fly into the side of her head. Searing pain shot through her and she toppled over, off the step and onto the pavement. Everything went black. She'd been knocked unconscious.

Sam witnessed the whole thing.

Apparently a girl they both knew from school called Rachel* had crept up behind them and jumped on her, punching and kicking her for no reason.

As Becky lay on the ground, the girl battered her with her fists.

'You stupid cow!' she screamed. 'You deserve everything you get.'

Sam begged the girl to stop. 'She's not done anything to you,' he told her. 'Just get off her!'

But Rachel wasn't listening. She started to stamp on her back, where her kidneys were. Amazingly, she even knew that Becky was born with only one kidney and that harming it could kill her.

*The name of the bully in this account has been changed.

Rachel wanted Becky dead. Becky's whole body was being beaten to a pulp. What was even worse was that there was a group of five boys from Becky's class standing by, just watching Rachel attack her.

That was when Sam noticed what was going on. Two of the boys, both aged sixteen, were filming the assault on their mobile phones.

'What are you doing?' Sam shouted at them. But the boys just laughed.

Becky was still unconscious and unaware of what was happening. Sam didn't know what to do and felt helpless at this point. Rachel had been beating Becky up for ten minutes by then, and was showing no signs of stopping.

Sam was just about to run for help when a classmate walked by and saw what was happening. Luckily, she had her mobile phone on her, so she called the ambulance immediately.

She then managed to pull Rachel off Becky.

'I've phoned the police,' she said to Rachel. 'Get off her.'

Rachel was scared off and she began running away with the rest of the group down the quiet street.

When the ambulance arrived a few minutes later, Becky was taken to North Manchester General

Hospital, where she had tests to make sure she had not been paralysed.

Doctors told her mother Becky was in a deep state of shock and suffered temporary paralysis, as well as being covered in bruises.

Becky had to stay at the hospital for two days to ensure she was healthy and had not suffered any lasting damage from the torrent of abuse she had received.

The next morning, when Becky woke up in her hospital bed, she felt very woozy. Her mother was sitting by her bedside.

'What happened, Mum?' she asked. Becky was confused and disoriented.

She held Becky's hand. 'You were beaten up,' she told her daughter. 'But you're safe now.'

She explained to Becky that Sam had witnessed the whole attack.

'It was a girl and some lads from your school,' she told Becky.

Becky could not believe what she was hearing.

The youths recorded the attack on a mobile video phone – a craze known as 'happy slapping'.

'Happy slapping' is the latest bullying phenomenon in which attacks, often random, are filmed on mobile phones then distributed among other phone users by the aggressors. Usually, the attacks involve one person slapping a passer-by or stranger while an accomplice films it with the telephone.

The videos can then be sent between phones and even posted on the Internet.

'Why did they do this to me?' she asked her mother.

She shook her head but did not answer. Tears rolled down her face.

X-rays showed that Becky had severe concussion and nerve damage to her leg, causing a condition known as foot drop.

Two days later, Becky was allowed home. But she was in so much pain that she could hardly walk. She had to use crutches and wear a special plastic shoe.

Greater Manchester Police were investigating the incident, but Becky was terrified. She felt trapped at home because she was too scared to go outside. Even a trip to the local corner shop sent a shiver down her spine – in case Rachel was waiting for her.

Her parents tried to stay strong and support their daughter, but her little brother Craig, who was only thirteen at the time, was very distraught.

The day after the attack on Becky, the video of her being beaten up was being circulated around school. Some pupils from Craig's class were watching it.

Craig was tricked into watching the clip. He was so disturbed by what he saw that he burst into tears and was immediately sent home from school on compassionate grounds.

'This is absolutely horrendous,' Becky's mother, Georgina, said at the time. 'They could have killed her. We're very lucky she's alive.

'But she won't go back to school because she's terrified, and now everyone's seen the video. The school should get rid of videophones, or are they going to wait until someone's been murdered before they take the phones off the kids?'

She also made a public plea to stop the video being circulated further.

Meanwhile, Plant Hill High School released a statement to the public. 'This is a police matter, which happened outside school,' a spokesman said.

Greater Manchester Police confirmed they were investigating the incident. 'We're appealing for information following an assault on a sixteen-year-old girl who suffered injuries to her head and body and was taken to hospital,' said a police spokesman. 'It's believed the offender ran off after the attack and we ask anyone with information to call us.'

Norman Brennan, director of the Victims of Crime Trust, said at the time that such assaults had to be taken seriously.

'This is not a bit of fun. It's a very serious crime. People can die from one punch,' he said.

The brutal assault on Becky Smith shocked the nation.

Within days, Greater Manchester Police said a girl from Blackley, Manchester, who could not be identified for legal reasons, had been arrested on suspicion of causing actual bodily harm after she went to a police station voluntarily.

But a spokeswoman added, 'Further to that we cannot comment.'

'I just want whoever did this to be caught. Becky was left in a hell of a state,' said Georgina.

But later that week a police spokesman announced that, on the advice of the Crown Prosecution Service, the girl would not be charged. She was given a final warning, the equivalent of a caution.

'I'm fuming,' Georgina said after hearing of the decision not to proceed with the charges. 'I couldn't believe what I was hearing. I thought they would make an example of her but instead she's free to walk around without a care in the world. What kind of a message does that send out to other youngsters?

'Becky's very angry about it. She's got to sit her last exam not knowing whether she's going to see this girl outside afterwards. She can't even go to the college she wants to because this girl is going there.'

She vowed to take out a private prosecution against the 'happy slap' attacker.

'It'll cost a bit of money, but it'll be worth it. As a parent you have to stand up and do as much as you can,' she said.

'She feels as if she's been beaten up and the girl who did it has got away with it. The police have slapped her again. She's done nothing wrong and doesn't deserve this,' she added.

'They've opened a door for other kids to do what they like and walk free. There's no deterrent to stop anyone else from doing the same. Maybe next time it'll be a murder, and then they'll have to do something about it, but it'll be too late by then.'

Those responsible for the attack, which included a girl and five boys, were also not expelled from Plant Hill High School.

Just three weeks after the attack, Becky had to sit her nine GCSEs. While the criminal investigation was proceeding, she sat them away from her classmates. But she was determined not to let her attackers affect her performance.

'Despite her ordeal, she hasn't lost her faith in human nature and the hundreds of cards and messages from friends, family and well-wishers had cheered her up,' Becky's mother says.

In the following weeks, some British schools banned mobile phones in an attempt to stamp out the craze. But Plant Hill High continued to allow their use at the school.

'This is a police matter, which happened outside school, and we're supporting the police with their inquiries,' a school spokesman said soon after.

The Victims of Crime Trust condemned the trend as a serious offence masquerading as entertainment.

'This is not a bit of fun. It is a very serious crime,' director Norman Brennan said. 'It's part of a society which has just about given up on law and order.'

At the time, Prime Minister Tony Blair made enforcing respect and civility on the street a priority for his government, which had taken office in 1997.

The British government said that it intended to set up task forces of expert teachers to tackle the problem of unruly behaviour in classrooms.

The then schools minister Jacqui Smith – who became Britain's first woman Home Secretary in June 2007 – said the new group would advise the government on how to improve discipline and how to get parents to accept responsibility for their children's behaviour.

'A culture of respect, good behaviour and firm discipline must be the norm in all schools all of the time,' she added.

## BEATING THE BULLIES

The 'happy slap' craze hit the headlines in May 2005 and has since brought a spate of assaults on innocent youngsters. Becky Smith's case was one of the worst.

Former Metropolitan Police Commissioner Lord Stevens called for tighter school discipline and the framing of new criminal offences to cover 'happy slap' attacks.

Anti-bullying organisations believe this teenage fad began in south London in late 2004 but has now spread across the country. It is an important part of the craze to record the look of utter shock on the victim after the initial blow.

The craze has been blamed on controversial television series which feature scenes involving the gratuitous infliction of pain and humiliation.

Metropolitan Police Commander Jim Smith also condemned the craze. 'I find it difficult to see how this can be fun or happy for anyone. Children who engage in criminal behaviour will be dealt with very strongly,' he said.

But, in 2006, compensation for Becky from the government was delayed after she was told that police from Grey Mare Lane Police station had 'no record' that the incident had been reported.

It was yet another blow for Becky and her family. Her mother Georgina was even more stunned to receive a letter from her solicitor, along with the letter from the Criminal Injuries Compensation Authority (CICA), claiming police had 'no record' of the incident.

She then spent days trying to find evidence that she reported the crime.

'I'm absolutely appalled. Everything seemed to be going smoothly, but then I got a letter saying that the police have no record that anything happened to her. What's going on?' Georgina said at the time.

'She spent time in hospital; she's been in all the papers; and now they have no record – it's ridiculous. She's been through enough as it is, without this,' she added.

A Greater Manchester Police spokesman later said that a clerical error had been made by the CICA, and this had been explained to Becky Smith's mother.

But Georgina says a lack of clear communication made the wait for compensation even harder.

'I called the CICA and they were laughing at the fact the police said they had no record of the incident because they had seen it all over the newspapers,' she said.

But Becky came out on top after passing all of her GCSE exams with flying colours – just three months after she had been viciously assaulted.

## BEATING THE BULLIES

The brave schoolgirl beat her bullies and she celebrated with a string of B grades.

'She's ecstatic. I went to collect them for her, as she was worried, but the school and her friends wished her all the best,' said Georgina.

Becky to this day does not understand why they chose her. Some of her friends say it is because Rachel was jealous of her. But that was no excuse.

But, for now, Becky wants to forget the attack and make a success of her life.

# 6

# Sebastian Sharp, 31

**W**alking along the rows of streets lined with perfect semidetached houses in Richmond, southwest London, fourteen-year-old Sebastian Sharp felt a distinct sense of dread as he reached the cold, metal gates at Shene School.

It was autumn of 1989.

Looking up at the school's clock, he took a deep breath and carried on walking. He knew this day would be no different from any other. He would need to be alert and avoid confrontation at all costs.

Sebastian's problems started in second year – two years before. Other pupils would often kick, punch, push and insult him for no apparent reason.

At the age of twelve, in 1988, he injured his leg

when he ran into a glass door fleeing a gang of boys trying to attack him.

Sebastian – who has three younger brothers, Oliver, Dominic and Benjamin – was used to having to be assertive, but around this gang he felt utterly powerless.

These boys also tore up his work, hit him across the head with rulers, threw things at him, tripped him up and jeered at him. By the end of his fifth year, he was tied up by classmates about twice a week.

The bullying seriously affected his personality, making him anxious, depressed and suicidal.

It all came to a head in 1991, when, aged fifteen, Sebastian ran away from home, leaving his parents a note saying he had been picked on and could not take any more.

His disappearance sparked a nationwide search with every news channel in the UK covering the story.

Four days later, he was found sleeping rough twenty miles from his home, shivering in his blue school uniform and a shell suit.

He finally cracked and told police he had been bullied. 'When I saw him at the police station, I said, "Why didn't you tell us? The first thing we would have done was have you out of that school," ' says Sebastian's mother, Janice Sharp.

Scores of previous incidents suddenly made sense to her. He had come home one day with his trousers ripped at the knee, and told his parents he had fallen off his bike, but, in fact, he had been thrown through the glass door.

'The string marks on his arms from when he was tied up were, he said at the time, from falling on the cord around a seeded area of grass.

'He was very communicative and would talk to us about every other subject. But he just held back from talking about school. We put it down to puberty,' she adds.

Her husband, Graham Sharp, said they were particularly angry about a school report two months before Sebastian disappeared, which gave no hint of the trauma he faced.

'On occasions, he finds other members of the group demanding and stressful. He is prepared to talk above this, and he responds in a mature way to these difficulties. He is well liked by the class,' stated the report.

While Sebastian was still missing, the family heard rumours that he had been bullied.

The local authority that runs the school, the London borough of Richmond, said the headmaster had investigated Sebastian's claims and found 'no substance' in them. But their son's disappearance prompted the Sharp family to contact anti-bullying groups for advice.

As a result, the family decided to take legal action and Sebastian launched a claim against his former school, stating that he had lost the best years of his life.

The family say they took legal action because they felt it was the only way to make the school realise the emotional and educational harm the bullying had caused in forcing him to move schools in the middle of his GCSE courses.

Sebastian claims the school was negligent because it failed to take reasonable care for his health and safety or to protect him from bullying.

He also alleges that it failed to respond adequately to his complaints. He demanded £200,000 compensation.

The case was due to be heard at the High Court in October 1996 and would have been a test of whether schools and their governors can be held responsible for failing to stop bullying.

It would also make legal history if he won, opening the gate for compensation for other children who say they have been victimised.

Richmond upon Thames council, which runs the school, said that it did not accept the allegations. In a statement the following day, it said all its secondary schools had 'clear and active policies against bullying'.

'The head teacher of Shene School, Simon Williams, carried out an internal investigation in 1991 following allegations made by Mr and Mrs Sharp and found no substance in the charges,' it read.

'Shene is a very popular, heavily over-subscribed school which enjoys an outstanding reputation for the quality of its care for all pupils. The school and the authority will be vigorously contesting the case.'

Cherie Booth, a Queen's Counsel and wife of the former Labour leader and Prime Minister Tony Blair, is an expert in family law, and was engaged by Jack Rabinowicz, the Sharps' solicitor, ten days before the High Court case was to begin.

'Our solicitors felt it would make the education authorities sit up a bit and it helped tremendously,' Janice Sharp said.

'She's an eminent QC in the field of education,' solicitor Jack Rabinowicz said soon afterwards.

'Mrs Blair was a lovely lady. I'm sure she helped us win,' Sebastian's father, Graham, aged forty-three, added.

Sebastian qualified for legal aid in bringing the action against the school governors.

He moved schools but performed badly in his

GCSEs, and felt unable to retake them because of continuing publicity.

It had also affected his job prospects after he had endured four unhappy years at the school, which he said made him anxious, depressed and suicidal.

'We say the school knew about it right from the start. There was one meeting where the kids were assembled and told they shouldn't do it, but it went on unabated, which gave Sebastian final despair,' said Jack Rabinowicz.

Sebastian claimed the school was negligent in failing to take reasonable care for his health and safety or protect him from bullying. The school admitted he had once complained of being called names but said this matter had been dealt with promptly.

Shene School decided not to contest this particular claim, but rejected Sebastian's original demand for £200,000 compensation. In the end, although the case was due to be heard at the High Court in London that month, it never came to a formal hearing.

Instead, the case was settled by the school's local education authority after insurers for Shene School offered the money in an out-of-court settlement.

'It is regrettable that this case got as far as the High Court,' said Paul King, the borough's vice-chairman of education. 'The school had a recent Ofsted inspection, which commended its policy on bullying. I would hope this will be an end to it, though we will never know whether there was any justice in his claim or whether the school was culpable.'

Simon Williams, head at the thousand-pupil comprehensive school, defended the borough's decision. 'The plaintiff had originally demanded £200,000 but the settlement was eventually for £33,000, which represents a considerable reduction,' he said.

'This action was legally aided. There were no risks faced by the plaintiff of incurring any financial costs and that must make schools vulnerable.

'There was one area when the pupil brought to the attention of his form tutor a problem about name-calling. We had an effective system for picking up these issues with a one-to-one session between pupil and tutor. The form tutor was an excellent teacher and had there been a serious problem then we would have picked up on it,' he added.

At the same time, government-backed research suggested that more than one in four primary schoolchildren and one in ten secondary school pupils were being bullied.

Support was also voiced by ChildLine at the time, the national free helpline for children, which said it was inundated by calls from bullying victims every year.

'This will give new hope to thousands of children who suffer bullying at school and to their parents,' a spokesman for the charity said.

'Thousands of children call ChildLine every year about being bullied, and in the past five years there has been an increase in the number of complaints about physical bullying.

'But, where the whole culture of the school is against bullying and teachers help children to understand that it is wrong, it can be nipped in the bud early.

'It is in schools which turn a blind eye to bullying and treat it as something that children should sort out on their own, where what begins as name-calling and teasing can rapidly escalate into outright physical violence.'

Upon hearing the news that he had won the out-of-court settlement, Sebastian celebrated his £33,000 payout.

Lawyers believed it was the first successful court case brought over bullying.

While newspaper journalists and television crews shouted requests for interviews through his letterbox that evening, six-foot Sebastian was holed up at his parents' terraced house in Richmond.

'Sebastian has been hiding in his bedroom all day,' said his mother Janice.

Neighbours described Sebastian as a quiet young man. 'He's a gentle lad who's always been good to me. It was obvious he wasn't very happy at school,' said Eileen Fitzgerald, who lives two doors away.

'I'm glad Sebastian's got the money. There's a lot of bullying going on at that school,' said thirteen-year-old Michelle Lane, who attended Shene School.

Sebastian later issued a statement through his parents. 'I hope from this that other children will get justice and realise they are not alone,' it read.

He also stated that he took legal action only 'to make schools answerable'.

'It's not just a success for Sebby, but for every other child,' added his father Graham Sharp.

'We spent five years doing this. It's a marvellous victory,' said his mother, Janice.

His parents said they had been to hell and back over the case. 'We're appalled and filled with sorrow that our son's lost all the best years of his life,' Janice told national Talk Radio that week. 'Teenage life should be a happy time. Our son can never get that back again. He's just rebuilding his life now.'

Bullied children must tell someone about the problem, they said, and they urged parents to act.

'For the parents that actually know, demand an immediate response from the school, and some action on what's going on in their school,' she added. 'If that doesn't work, take it higher to the education authority, and, if all else fails, you've got to seek further advice from somebody else.'

It is thought the case could lead to hundreds of similar actions. But Janice warned that pursuing the legal route was not easy. 'We're just ordinary people. To take on something like this is awe-inspiring,' she said.

'It's not easy, you only get this far if you have a case, and there's a case to answer, and because of the severity of the case we've gone through hell and back, actually.'

Although Sebastian says he will never fully recover from his four years of being bullied, he is trying to rebuild his life. He now works as a clerk at a London stockbroker and has taken up boxing in an attempt to toughen himself up.

# 7

# Caroline Stillman, 14

One Friday evening in late January 2006, thirteen-year-old Caroline Stillman was in her bedroom talking to her elder brother and sister online when a new member popped up on her screen.

The intruder, whom Caroline knew slightly at school, asked for her name. She gave it.

'F***ing lanky bitch!' came the response.

Caroline was and six foot three tall. She was away from Uppingham Community College, a co-educational school in Rutland for 850 eleven-to-sixteen-year-olds.

Now even this sanctuary had been invaded by her tormentors. She ran downstairs to her mother, Sarah, and wept.

After a brief discussion, the two of them went back upstairs. While Sarah stood by as moral support, Caroline sat down at the computer to draw out her tormentor – first asking her whether she would feel equally justified in being rude to someone who was short or black or disabled.

The exchange is still on Caroline's computer – a litany of crass insults that include 'Trampy bitch', 'f***ing dumb ass bitch', 'ugly lanky giant' and, finally, 'Go kill yourself lanky bitch.'

When Caroline showed a printout of this venomous attack to her father, Bill, he was so appalled that he called the chairman of the school governors, asking for the headmaster, Malcolm England, to call him back. England, however, advised that the matter was outside the school's jurisdiction and suggested that Bill Stillman take whichever course he thought was necessary.

Caroline's father rang the police.

Meanwhile, Caroline dug out a list she had typed of all the bullying incidents she could remember. They covered three sheets of A4 – a shocking testimony to how cruel adolescents can be.

A sad postscript says, 'I cannot write all of it down because there have been so many that I can't remember all of them.'

The three-page list included the following.

- A girl called me a giraffe in the dinner hall and said to her friends: 'I f***ing swear she's a giraffe.'
- A boy chased me around the classroom with a saw.
- A boy in maths called me a tree and said I couldn't do maths because trees can't speak.
- A group of girls held me down on the table in Humanities and stuck chewing-gum in my hair.
- A particular person called me a giant and said they were scared of me.
- Two girls called me names and made me cry and run out of the classroom.
- A girl asked me as I got off the bus if my mum was a lanky bitch like me.
- A boy tried to poke me with his scissors.
- A group of girls constantly threatened to beat me up.
- Two girls whispered things under their breath as I was trying to answer a question out loud in French. I gave up and cried.

For Caroline, this was not just random abuse: it was the culmination of two and a half years of torment for being exceptionally tall.

Most of that time, she had coped with the bullying at school because she had felt safe at home.

At six foot three, she towers over her parents,

who are both six feet. She was only an inch shorter in September 2004, when she arrived for her first day at Uppingham Community College at the age of eleven.

Neither at home nor at primary school had she ever been teased because of her height, so she was looking forward to five years in the school.

Her enthusiasm, however, was short-lived. As she entered the gates, she heard a girl call out 'lanky bitch' in a loud voice.

'From that day onwards, a day didn't pass without someone saying something horrible to me about my height,' she says.

To begin with, it was just name-calling.

Other girls would call out: 'giraffe', 'lollipop stick', 'giant', 'elephant' – indifferent to the fact that Caroline suffers from Marfan syndrome, a chromosomal disorder that affects the connective tissue and can cause heart and eye problems as well as exceptional growth.

People with the Marfan syndrome are typically, but not always, very tall or taller than unaffected people in their family, slender and loose-jointed.

'On that first day, I came home from school and went to my room,' she remembers. 'I didn't say anything until much later, when my mother found me crying. I told her what had happened but I begged her not to go into the school to sort it out – I didn't want to make things worse by making a fuss.

'After that, I would be moody and silent in the evenings. I knew it was unfair to take it out on Mum, but I suppose I was punishing her for sending me to that school.'

The family's modern home in the rolling countryside of Rutland, just a few minutes from the school, is not adapted for the very tall, so Caroline's head nearly scrapes the top of the door frames.

Otherwise, the only special provisions for height are extra-long beds and baths, which have long been necessary because Caroline's elder brother, Samuel, who also suffers from Marfan syndrome, is six foot eight.

At school, no one was interested in finding out what it felt like to be tall, and Caroline was not the kind of sporty type who could use her height to become the secret weapon of the basketball team.

Instead, it made her a butt of jokes.

The same thing had happened to another girl: Morgan Mussen, a six-foot thirteen-year-old from Nottingham in England. She died after taking an overdose of painkillers in 2001 because she could not face the school bullies.

In line with school policy, Caroline told her form

tutor about the name-calling – the first of several complaints.

'I was always asked what I had been doing to provoke the bullies. I said that I hadn't done anything – that's why it was bullying. Sometimes, the teacher would tell the bullies not to speak to me, but that meant I was isolated. Anyway, it always started up again,' she says.

By the second term of Year Seven, Caroline's mother was feeling uneasy about her daughter. A gentle, motherly woman, she had been wary of interfering too soon, because of her own experiences as an unusually tall adolescent.

She, too, had been called names at school.

'It damaged my confidence,' she says. 'But I got through, probably because I had a couple of good friends and the school acted quickly.

'My elder daughter had been called "a man" because she played football and my son had been called "giant", but they had coped – so I hoped Caroline would, too.'

But, after six months, she knew she had to act.

By then, her daughter was refusing to go into town after school for fear of meeting other pupils, or hiding in the car when they went shopping. Worse, still, Caroline confessed that the unkind name-calling had now turned into threats.

'At the end of form time in our classroom,' Caroline says, 'a girl said to me, "You walk funny." I left the classroom to go downstairs for break. But, as I was going down the concrete stairs, several girls gathered round me and one put her foot between my legs to trip me up, saying, "Lanky bitch!"'

It was the tipping point for Caroline's parents. Her mother went straight in to see Caroline's teacher, who assured her the situation would be dealt with. But the attacks continued.

On one occasion, Caroline was in a history lesson sitting at a table when two girls held her shoulders and pushed her back on a table while another stuck chewing gum in her hair.

'The whole class was laughing. I do not know whether the teacher heard or not, but after the lesson, as I walked out, she asked if I was OK,' she says.

Yet it was not until Year Eight, when four girls threatened to beat her up during break time, that Caroline went to the headmaster for the first time – chiefly because his office was nearby.

'I'll talk to them next week,' was his response.

She was so frightened that she spent the rest of the break quivering in the loo.

Thereafter, she would spend all her breaks hiding in the library, but there were still the corridors to contend with.

**79**

The attacks were of two different types. The persistent sneers and gibes came from a pack of girls, led by two individuals. The physical threats came from a pupil in her design-technology class, who would try to shoo her away by poking her with scissors, waving a saw at her or threatening her with a hammer – on one occasion, he hit her with it.

Caroline felt unable ever to relax.

Then, in September 2006 at the beginning of Year Nine, it got worse. Until then, she had had one or two allies, but the bullies took them to the loos and told them not to speak to her. Friendless, she developed headaches and sore throats at the prospect of school and began to be sick after every meal.

It was after one of those family meals that month that Bill finally realised the seriousness of what was happening to his daughter.

'When she talked about being sick,' he says, 'I thought she meant she was just coughing up a little phlegm. But one day, after dinner, I happened to go upstairs to the bathroom and found the evidence in the basin.'

Until then, Sarah Stillman had handled the matter, leaving her husband to run his advertising and marketing business. But now he took over. He took Caroline to their GP, who said they had 'a very depressed girl' on their hands and signed her off sick from school.

Bill was adamant that she should not return to school this term, although Malcolm England – by then fully in the picture – told him that the bullies had been dealt with.

'The bullies do it because they can get away with it,' Bill said at the time. 'I brought my children up properly, though some have criticised me for it.'

'I cannot discuss an individual student,' England said shortly afterwards. 'We are aware of the problems facing this student and her family, both within and outside the school.

'Professional support has been sought and we hope that our combined efforts will prove effective in ensuring a successful return to school. The school needs to tackle these things openly and, if you stand up to them, bullies can be sorted out.'

But, at this stage, it was too late for Caroline to consider returning to the school.

The Stillman family thought about sending her to a private school because of the more radical action that is taken to protect children against bullying. But they could not afford the fees.

While they decided what to do, Caroline was being educated at home and gradually regaining her confidence.

'It has really lowered my confidence and scared me and I'm really worried about having to go back. Whenever I think about it I feel sick,' she said at the time.

Her mother said, 'My daughter isn't having the education she's entitled to. But we don't feel it's safe for her to go back to that school. We can't see that changing unless there's a total overhaul of what's going on there.'

'I've cried, my wife's cried, and the whole thing has been an emotional upset,' Bill Stillman added.

Meanwhile, Inspector Adam Streets from Leicestershire Constabulary said that officers were investigating a complaint of harassment and bullying and that anyone found responsible would be prosecuted.

'We are treating this very seriously,' he said at the time.

The Crown Prosecution Service was also busy sifting through her case to decide whether to bring charges against the bullies.

The messages of support she received from other bullied pupils after she left gave Caroline renewed faith. Even more importantly, she has heard from others with Marfan syndrome as a result.

'I know I'm not alone now,' she says.

Her ordeal also struck a chord with parents

throughout the country. And an anti-bullying organisation called Stop Bullying Me took up her cause and offered to help. They immediately faxed through details of Caroline's case to Prime Minister Tony Blair, members of the Shadow Cabinet and the Liberal Democrat party.

Tony Blair responded in a letter and said the information had been passed on to the appropriate government department for action.

'I'm very glad to hear from the Prime Minister's office,' Bill Stillman said. 'The chairman of Marfan Organisation UK kindly has also written to Uppingham Community College principal Malcolm England, the director of education Carol Chambers and MP Alan Duncan on the family's behalf,' he added.

He said his daughter had been offered ten hours a week of home tuition in maths, English and science. But, for now, Caroline is determined to get back into the classroom.

'I'd like to go back to that school, but obviously not with those bullies still there. I'd just really like to get an education,' she says.

But, above all, Caroline is happy that she is finally being listened to.

'Now I want to help other kids from being bullied,' she says.

# 8

# Sophie Parks, 19

On a bleak, windswept afternoon on the Isle of Lewis in the Hebrides, nineteen-year-old Sophie Parks's eyes flash over the rolling green hills as she recalls the ordeal she went through for almost two years.

Sophie is so slight and pale she is almost ethereal, a feature only accentuated by smudged grey circles into the fine, translucent skin under her eyes.

The fragility of her physical appearance is, however, deceptive. For Sophie is assertive and articulate as well as intelligent.

It was March 2003 when Sophie and her mother Sally, aged forty-six, moved from Matlock in Derbyshire to Lewis. Mother and daughter had spent the two previous summers on the island, visiting friends, and Sally loved its remote beauty. Some of the most beguiling scenery in the Hebrides and a vast array of wildlife can be found on the Isle of Lewis. Sophie, however, was less enthusiastic.

'It's not exactly what you want when you're fourteen. I felt Lewis was pretty... but boring,' says Sophie.

Despite the attractions of island life, the reality of living in a remote community can be far tougher than expected – especially for teenagers.

But Sally Parks thought the Scottish education system would be superior and enrolled Sophie at the Nicolson Institute in Stornoway. Sophie was surprised when she settled easily into island life.

As mother and daughter settled into their new house with a breathtaking view over the loch in the village of Balallan and Sally bought Sophie a pony called Prince, the teenager quickly made friends – both island-born and English incomers.

For nine months all went well.

But, when Sophie, then fifteen, entered her third year at the institute, things began to change. From then on, the reality of life on Lewis was shockingly different from the dream.

In January 2004, a misunderstanding with the fellow Nicolson pupil occurred – a girl Sophie claims was often in trouble.

It was then that the vicious assaults and racist taunts began.

'It started with something really petty with this one girl, then she came up to me in the school hall and just head-butted me,' says Sophie.

'Sophie was not withdrawn, but she was snappy and I didn't know what was wrong,' admits Sally. 'One day she turned round to me and said, "How would you like to be smashed in the face?"'

With Sally's encouragement, Sophie went straight to the teachers.

'But nobody did a thing, so I just walked out of school and went down to my local police station,' says Sophie.

That was a bold move for a fifteen-year-old. But Sophie felt that she was entitled to protection.

'At least the police were sympathetic,' she says.

The police already knew this girl. She had been in trouble before. But, because the girl was under sixteen, the police were powerless to act.

Sally Parks decided to speak to the school headmaster herself but nothing improved.

In the coming months, there were six attacks on Sophie from this one girl alone. Sophie was not only repeatedly attacked by this girl but also by the girl's friends.

## BEATING THE BULLIES

On one occasion, two friends of the main tormentor – both a year older than Sophie – beat her so badly that she damaged her kidneys and was coughing up blood.

Sophie had to be taken by ambulance to the hospital. The police investigated the attack but nobody was charged.

'The bullies were this popular in-group at school,' says Sophie. 'This girl was always most likely to attack me when she had an audience. That's what she got off on.'

'I had tried my best to fit in but I couldn't choose where I was born,' Sophie says.

But Sophie clearly hated feeling like a victim. She tried to fight back. On one occasion, she was disciplined by a teacher for hitting two girls back after they attacked her.

Sophie admits that eventually the bullying closed her life down. Most days, she was too scared to attend classes.

For a confident, fun-loving girl who liked nothing more than to go for long walks amid the beautiful scenery of the Outer Hebrides, the dream of living on an island had turned completely sour for Sophie. She became a virtual prisoner in her own home, refusing to go out.

'It got so bad that I wouldn't go into town

unless I had friends with me. I didn't have much of a life,' she says.

Some of her close friends even started to avoid her because they were scared of being singled out, too.

Her mother was also targeted by the bullies. She received threatening phone calls, was heckled and had a lit cigarette thrown at her face when she tried to protect her daughter in the street.

At one point, the bullying got so bad that Sophie even contemplated suicide.

'She's a tough little nut but the only thing that stopped her taking tablets was the thought that my dad would have a heart attack and that would impact on my mother and me,' says Sally.

Sophie did not want to let the bullies win.

'It was awful, it was mob-handed, it was just disgraceful,' said Sophie's mother. 'The bullying really affected her emotionally. They would regularly say to her, "You don't belong here."'

It even got to the stage where two teachers had to walk Sophie to the bus terminal.

'How embarrassing is that when you're fifteen!' says Sophie. 'I started drinking,' she admits. 'That's common on Lewis. Three or four kids – as young as thirteen – buy a litre of vodka between them and drink it down the pier or in the castle grounds or at older friends' houses. There's not much else to do. I was just so unhappy.'

Sophie is not your stereotypical bully's victim.

'She's got a very strong personality,' says Sally. 'In normal circumstances, she would be able to take care of herself.'

But the events taking place on Lewis were far from normal.

'If I had been an adult and this had taken place in the workplace it would have been harassment,' says Sophie.

'This is a beautiful, breathtaking place, but living on Lewis isn't easy if you're not from here. There are some lovely people here, but they close ranks if you're an outsider. I had this dream about what island life would be like, and it wasn't like that at all.'

In fact, twelve-year-old Molly Campbell attended the same school before fleeing the Western Isles to live with her father in Pakistan, sparking an international custody battle. Molly, also known as Misbah Rana, alleged she too suffered racial abuse in Stornoway.

At the time, much had been made in the media of the anti-English taunts that were integral to the bullying.

'I don't think you could call the bullying racially

motivated exactly,' says Sophie. 'It was more that they used the race thing as a tool.

'However, there is racism among adults on Lewis. They are racist about all outsiders, but particularly about the English. It's the same in school. There are a lot of English people on the island and the islanders have English friends, but, the moment there's a fallout, it's English this or that.'

Of the claims about anti-English prejudice on Lewis, Sally says some islanders really welcome outsiders – and others don't.

'There's no in-between,' she says.

Sophie and her mother claim Western Isles Council was told repeatedly about the bullying but nothing changed.

'One of the bullies was suspended from school twice, but apart from that they were just told off, given a slap on the hand,' says Sophie.

A council spokesman refused to comment on the possibility of legal action, but said that it sought to provide a 'safe environment' for all pupils.

Sally Parks and her daughter then had several meetings with the council, as Sophie hoped to transfer to Sir Edward Scott's School at Tarbert, Harris, to sit her Highers (school-leaving exams in Scotland) – just thirty minutes away. But, when she asked it to fund her daughter's travel costs, the request was turned down.

A council spokesman said, 'The school is of the view that they can provide a safe environment. Therefore, while it's up to parents to make a placing request, we believe that the school is safe and there is no reason to change the terms of the policy not to pay the cost of transport.'

He said the instances of bullying were investigated and disciplinary measures had been taken.

In the end, the situation was an educational disaster for Sophie. She did not attend school for the last three months of her standard-grade year, and even before that her attendance was patchy.

Despite everything, Sophie still managed to pass five A–C grades, including an A for English, in her GCSEs in the summer of 2005.

She eventually decided that the only way to escape her ordeal was by leaving the island altogether, even though this meant parting from her mother.

'I left school as soon as I could,' she says. 'I cried because it was hard to leave my mum, but I just couldn't stay.'

Sophie moved in with her grandparents, Shirley and Jack Watson, near Sheffield, South Yorkshire, in August 2005 and moved to a college in nearby Chesterfield to study fabrication and welding.

Sally Parks, who works as a domestic assistant for the local health board, could not afford to make the move to Sheffield and remained in Lewis, six hundred miles away from her daughter.

'We're never going to see each other. I can't afford to make the journey regularly and neither can my parents. They're both in their seventies and living off my dad's pension,' she said at the time.

'It was so painful the day Sophie left, she was so distraught that the plane couldn't take off straightaway,' she added.

In the year after Sophie left Lewis, she had been back only once, and she admitted at the time that even on holiday she was scared she might bump in to one of her old tormenters.

Then, in the summer of 2006, Sally decided to follow her daughter out of Lewis. She sold her house and moved to the mainland. But Sophie is still angry about her time at the institute.

'I still feel it was just so unfair that I had to put up with it and that I had to leave my mum,' she says. 'I wouldn't want anyone else to have to go through the same thing. I get so angry thinking about what happened.'

Sophie sat her standard-grade exams at the

school in 2006, achieving top grades. She plans to go to university to study electrical engineering.

Sophie and Sally Parks are actively taking legal advice to see if they have a case to bring against Western Isles Council for not doing more to protect Sophie during her time at the school.

Sally Parks said at the time that she wanted to prevent anyone else suffering such treatment. 'We just don't want to see this happen to anyone else,' she said.

Western Isles Council said that no one was available to comment on the matter.

Whatever the truth about Nicolson's response to the bullying, the council spokesman, Nigel Scott, insisted there were robust anti-bullying policies in place in all the authority's schools, including the Nicolson Institute.

'There isn't a school in Scotland that can guarantee bullying won't occur,' he says. 'But what schools can do is put robust procedures and policies in place and we are confident we have done that. In fact, the Nicolson Institute's bullying policies were commended in a Schools Inspectorate report last year.'

Of the allegations of anti-English prejudice, Scott said that Lewis is home to many English families and people from many other backgrounds.

'I know English people here who wouldn't dream of living anywhere else,' he says. 'We are not immune to problems, but perhaps we get more attention because people think that sort of thing can't happen on an island.'

But Sophie and her mother decided they wanted to take legal action against the Western Isles council. Sophie was keenly following a test case of a schoolgirl called Natalie King, who was suing Aberdeen City Council for £20,000 over its alleged failure to protect her from bullies.

Sophie's final decision about suing the Western Isles council depended on the outcome of that case.

'I want to push ahead with it [legal action] partly because I don't want it to happen to anyone else but mainly because I feel the way I was treated by the council and the school wasn't fair,' she says.

Although Natalie King dropped her case in the end, Sophie wants to keep fighting her corner. If Sophie starts court proceedings it will be the first case of its kind at the Court of Session in Edinburgh. If successful, it could open the floodgates for another thirty similar cases.

'I want my day in court,' she says. 'I just want some justice.'

Note: There was no date set for the court case as this book was being prepared.

# 9

# Kirsty Perkins, 14

Strolling along the warm sandy beach one summer evening in 2004, twelve-year-old Kirsty Perkins was enjoying some quality time with her mother, Marie.

With its rolling green hills and tranquil sea, the country of Gwynedd, in northwest Wales, was the picture of beauty.

It was the end of the summer holidays and Kirsty was due to start Ysgol Glan Clwyd in a few days (*ysgol* means 'school' in Welsh).

As parents sat talking on the benches, watching their children playing ball games by the sea, Kirsty's thoughts turned to her new school.

'Mummy, will I make friends at ysgol?' she asked her mother.

Sensing her daughter's nerves, Marie wrapped her arm around Kirsty's shoulder.

'Don't worry,' she told her. 'You'll be just fine.'

Kirsty was comforted by her mother's warm words and her anxiety turned to excitement.

When Kirsty started at Ysgol Glan Clwyd shortly afterwards, she found the transition from primary to secondary school easy. She got on well with her new teachers and made friends with the other girls in her class.

The first few months at the school flew by quickly.

'I love it!' she told her mother in February 2005, just five months after starting.

But, just one month later, the atmosphere between her and the other girls in her class began to change.

'Don't you think you should stop eating so much?' one of the girls told her in the canteen one day.

Kirsty was shocked. This girl's remark had come completely out of the blue.

Just a few days later, a group of boys and girls walked past her the school corridor.

'Fatty!' they all called, laughing and pointing at Kirsty.

Kirsty ran to the bathroom and burst into tears.

She could not understand why they had suddenly turned on her. After that, it got even worse.

By April, a group of girls from her year started putting images of her on the networking site MySpace, a free service that uses the Internet for online communication through an interactive network of photos, blogs, user profiles, email, web forums and groups, as well as other media formats.

The pictures were of Kirsty with 'Fat Cow' written next to them. When a friend of Kirsty's from primary school discovered the images accidentally, she told Kirsty immediately.

'I was horrified,' says Kirsty. 'It was so humiliating.'

She told her parents about the photos that evening.

'Right,' Marie told her daughter. 'You must tell your teachers first thing tomorrow morning.'

Kirsty took her mother's advice and spoke to her headteacher. He assured the schoolgirl that he would take action.

'My teacher had a word with the girls,' says Kirsty. 'But it wasn't enough to make them stop picking on me.'

For the next few months, the girls continued to attack Kirsty verbally on a daily basis.

Just one year later, in early 2004, the bullying had become intolerable for Kirsty.

'I felt there was no one here to help me,' she says. 'I thought my only way out of this misery was to kill myself.'

That evening, she swallowed half a box of painkillers. Upon finding her daughter asleep on her bed at 7 p.m., her mother called out to wake her.

'Kirsty? Kirsty?' she said in a loud voice. 'Come on, you've got homework to do!'

But Kirsty did not wake up. Marie rushed over to shake her.

'Oh, my God!' she shouted. 'Ian, it's Kirsty, come quick!'

Upon hearing the commotion, Kirsty's father ran into the room. When he saw his young daughter lying next to a packet of painkillers, he knew instantly what she had done.

'Get an ambulance now!' he shouted at Marie, cradling her apparently lifeless body.

Kirsty was rushed to a nearby hospital, where her stomach was pumped. It was only then that Marie and Ian realised the severity of what had been happening to their daughter.

'We can't let this happen again,' Ian told his wife. 'She's our child – we have to protect her from now on.'

When Kirsty eventually woke up in the hospital bed, she felt a huge sense of guilt.

'When I look back and think what could have happened to me, I get very upset because I was so selfish,' she says. 'I could have hurt other people, people I love, by killing myself.'

'But she was scared and alone,' says Marie. 'She thought it was her only choice.'

Kirsty recovered from her ordeal, and, with the help of a close friend from primary class, soon felt strong enough to go back to class.

When she returned to class, Kirsty hoped that the girls would feel guilty for having inflicted so much pain on another human being.

'I hoped they would leave me alone after that,' she says.

But, just a few weeks later, the bullying reached a new low.

'You know there's a picture of you on Bebo,' a classmate told her one day.

Kirsty was bemused.

That evening, she went home and logged onto Bebo, a popular Internet forum.

'I was horrified,' she says. 'I almost fell of my chair.'

It was a digitally altered image mocking Kirsty's suicide attempt. It showed a picture of a graveyard and Kirsty with a knife against her head and a caption saying, 'I Love Suicide'.

She knew these girls hated her, but their campaign had just been taken to new lengths.

'I was so upset,' she says. 'It brought back very painful memories.'

Enraged, Kirsty contacted the Bebo webmaster to report the incident. The offending pictures were immediately removed by the site regulator. But the webmaster said that they were powerless to take any action against the girls who posted the image.

'What I couldn't believe was that I got a warning from the webmaster for swearing online because I was angry about what was being put up about me,' she adds.

But Kirsty's anger fuelled a side of Kirsty's personality she had not encountered before: her fighting spirit.

'I decided I wanted to fight,' she says. 'I wanted to make sure nobody else had to go through the suffering I'd been through.'

That day, Kirsty contacted local media to tell them about her ordeal at the hands of bullies. She urged every bullied child in Britain to speak out.

'I would tell victims to keep strong and tell someone who can help,' she says. 'I felt scared and ashamed about being bullied. My mum was upset when I told her. She couldn't get her head around it.

But it made such a big difference to talk to someone about it.'

She also highlighted the fact that many schoolchildren were being bullied.

'There are lots of kids out there going through the same thing. There's probably a few in my school because of the size of it. People who are being bullied are scared because they feel that if they do anything or say anything it'll make things worse.

'But it doesn't have to be like that. You have to say something. What people have to remember is that the bullies are the cowards, not the people being bullied. They are the ones who are scared. We're stronger than they are and they can't do anything to hurt us,' she added.

She also spoke out against websites such as Bebo. 'I believe they are being misused by bullies,' she told local press. 'These websites should be shut down. It's just not fair on the people being bullied out there. Kids are using these websites to bully other people – not to put up their homepages or do anything useful with.'

Later that week, Kirsty's father Ian and mother Marie met the school's headmaster to discuss the Internet postings.

'The Gwynedd Schools Service is aware that material about a pupil at the school was posted on this website and that the material has subsequently been removed,' said a Gwynedd Council spokesman.

The spokesman also confirmed pupils were blocked from accessing Bebo.com during school hours. But he said it was difficult for schools to take disciplinary action if the posting happened outside school hours.

Meanwhile, Marie said she was 'extremely proud' of her daughter for speaking out publicly. 'We didn't know anything was going on at the beginning,' she told media. 'She felt she couldn't talk to anybody for a long time. But the things put on this website were atrocious, absolutely atrocious.

'I don't think parents always realise what goes on with these websites. They're hidden away, out of sight. It often takes something really drastic for parents to realise what's going on and for the problem to sink in.'

Since its launch in July 2005, more than 26 million people have logged onto Bebo.

The largest site of its kind in the UK, it was set up so school, university and college friends could chat together online.

But the site has come under fire for allowing strangers to alter a user's personal page – as in Kirsty's case.

In 2006 measures were finally introduced to clamp down on bullying. Users must now approve any changes to their homepages – meaning offensive images such as those found by Kirsty cannot be placed on the website.

'Sadly, children face risks in everyday life, whether playing in their school grounds or on the internet,' said a Bebo spokesman. 'We are very conscious of this and are working hard to ensure our site is not abused.

'With that in mind, we introduced an anti-bullying initiative... as a further measure to address online bullying – something we will not tolerate on our site. Users can now opt to pre-screen comments and images that others attempt to post to their Bebo homepage.'

Schoolchildren across the UK can also learn how to stay safe on the Internet in a government-backed child-protection project. The Child Exploitation and Online Protection Centre (CEOP) launched its first nationwide education programme in 2006 at its London office.

Officials hope the ThinkuKnow campaign will make children think more about whom they are chatting to online. The talks and workshops will be delivered by police, child-protection specialists, social services and teachers in schools.

## BEATING THE BULLIES

CEOP also serves to highlight the first online police facility for children to report abuse on the official website. Home Office minister Vernon Coaker was present at the launch, alongside CEOP's chief executive Jim Gamble.

'The Web is a great place to have fun and meet new people, and millions of children across the UK are online every day chatting, social-networking and playing interactive games. But, where children go, child-sex predators will follow,' said a CEOP spokesman.

The centre, affiliated to the Serious Organised Crime Agency (SOCA), said one in twelve children who make contact with someone on the Internet will go to meet them in person.

The director of the anti-bullying charity Bullying Online, Liz Carnell, said youngsters should not be afraid to speak out. She said the charity was swamped with complaints about sites such as Bebo.

'We're getting a lot of complaints about Bebo and similar sites like MySpace at the moment,' she said. 'When people put their details on a website they're often putting themselves at risk of malevolent people ready to post abuse about them.

'What I would say to anyone out there who's being bullied over the Internet is that it's not difficult for the police to track down who puts these things online. What we do find is that people who have these problems are reluctant to come forward because they're afraid of being stopped from using the Internet at home.

'Generally though, it's very important children come forward and tell someone, whether it's to parents or friends or whoever,' Liz added.

Kirsty said, 'I think this is a very good idea and is definitely the sort of thing I would use.'

Kirsty had to face some of the most gutless and cruel personal attacks on the Internet. But she can take great comfort from the knowledge that her tormentors were so lacking in personal courage that they had to hide behind the anonymity of a website.

But she is the winner.

'The only way to deal with bullies is to stand up to them – for they are invariably cowards as well,' she said.

Kirsty now urges everyone who has been – or is being, or in future becomes – the so-called victim of bullying to remember her story and take comfort and strength from it. They should also – as Kirsty has done – tell the people who love them.

'Because there is no need to fight the bullies alone, and there is nothing to be ashamed of,' she says.

Now more than ever, Kirsty is determined to beat

the bullies. 'Knowing I could stand up for myself
gave me my confidence back,' she says.

# 10

# Michael Shanley, 47

Ironing the last of the creases from his dark-blue uniform, Michael Shanley's devoted wife Angela prepared breakfast for her husband and two children at their home in County Sligo, in northwest Ireland.

It was 1991 and Michael's first day as a fireman at a Sligo fire station. He had enjoyed his last few years at another fire unit in the county, but wanted a change of scenery.

As he walked inside the building, past the large red vehicles and array of machinery, he made his way towards the office. He was looking forward to the prospect of meeting his new workmates.

'You must be the new guy.' One man in his late

fifties jumped up from his seat upon seeing Michael pass through the kitchen area.

'Yeah, I'm Michael Shanley,' he replied.

Four other colleagues then got up to greet Michael.

'It's good to have a new guy around,' they told him, shaking his hand one by one.

Michael instantly fitted in well with his work-mates and looked forward to starting his first assignment.

Later that day, he finally met his boss – Station Officer Liam O'Donnell. From that moment onwards, Michael's expectations of his new job changed completely.

'You new, then?' he grunted aggressively at Michael, in front of his colleagues. It was clear that Liam O'Donnell liked to exert his control over all members of his team. But Michael tried to remain unfazed.

As he set off that afternoon on a local mission, his thoughts turned to Liam O'Donnell.

'I started to dread what he would be like to work with,' Michael admits.

But during the course of the next few weeks, Michael could not have predicted what Liam O'Donnell had in store for him.

'You stupid p***k,' Liam O'Donnell shouted at Michael one morning. 'You'd better get that toilet cleaned or you'll have hell to pay.'

Michael was then made to perform the demeaning task of cleaning the station toilets – instead of the duties he was assigned upon commencing his employment.

When he returned home that evening, he opened up to his wife, Angela.

'My boss is a real tyrant,' he told her. 'I'm not sure what to do about him.'

Angela advised him to keep calm and continue as usual. But, by the following week, O'Donnell was still making Michael perform cleaning tasks.

'Aren't you meant to be helping us put out fires?' one of his work colleagues asked him shortly afterwards.

Michael was relieved that someone had noticed.

'Yeah, what can I do about it?' he replied sarcastically.

Michael did not want to confront the issue openly in front of his colleagues unless O'Donnell found out.

'I sensed that Liam would make my life fifty times worse if he found out,' Michael later admitted.

During the course of the next few months, Liam O'Donnell subjected Michael to daily intimidation. While all the other firemen at the Sligo Fire Station saw Michael as an excellent officer who handled them well, O'Donnell was determined to stain his reputation.

He went about this by spreading rumours about Michael. It was an attempt to isolate him from his colleagues. Although it did not have the desired effect on his workmates, by this time Michael was at breaking point.

After a nonstop series of false accusations were made against him, Michael's morale sank to new depths.

'I contemplated suicide,' he admits.

He returned home one evening and thought seriously about ending his life. He thought it was the only way out of the misery he was suffering at the hands of Liam O'Donnell.

'I pulled myself together for the sake of my family,' says Michael. 'But I was very close to ending it all.'

When Michael returned to work, the abuse carried on as usual. Day after day, he was verbally attacked.

'W****r!' O'Donnell would shout at Michael. 'You're rubbish at your job.'

But O'Donnell was a very clever bully. He made sure he hid the abuse by hardly ever taunting Michael in front of witnesses.

False accusations continued to be made against Michael regarding his private and professional life. The threats got so bad that Michael even began to fear for his safety at Sligo fire station – scared that O'Donnell would try to harm him physically as well as mentally.

Despite this, Michael still managed to retain a good relationship with all his other colleagues, who saw him as an excellent officer.

Over the course of the next few years, Michael's personality changed drastically as a result of the abuse. He had always been an open, trusting person, but, after suffering at the hands of Liam O'Donnell, he began to find it difficult to hold a conversation with anyone.

Often reduced to tears by the treatment he received, he lost his trust in people and became negative and withdrawn.

'I was good at my work and wanted to stay in the job,' he says. 'It was my life.'

By 1996, five years after the abuse first started, Michael had become a father for the second time.

'But I was so caught up in trying to survive at the fire station that I missed out on years of rearing my children,' he says.

His marital life was also about to suffer greatly. Around that time, his wife Angela suffered a serious brain tumour and was very ill for a long period.

But, despite trying his hardest, Michael was unable to concentrate fully on his wife's illness due to the abuse he was receiving from Liam O'Donnell, who was still using obscene language towards Michael and threatening him.

Michael filed numerous complaints over the years to his superiors, but nothing happened.

Finally, after years of cruelty with no support from his employers, and with his physical and mental health suffering badly, Michael decided he had had enough.

He had always prided himself on being a family man, but now his family was suffering as a result.

The final straw came after Michael returned from a family holiday in 1999. He had just spent two idyllic weeks abroad with his wife and children, now he would have to come back and deal with Liam O'Donnell again.

On his return to Ireland, Michael felt a huge knot in his stomach and could sense that he was spiralling into a state of depression again. Then, upon hearing that the chief fire officer and assistant chief officer had the day off, he began seriously to fear for his own safety. He started to imagine the threats that Liam O'Donnell would hurl at him.

'It's consuming you,' Angela told him. 'Please, you've got to do something.'

At that moment, Michael cracked. The years of

repeated maltreatment and torment had finally made taken their toll.

'I didn't want my family ruined because it,' he says.

Instead, he contacted his local union branch and explained to them what had been happening to him. On their advice, he then took his case to the Trinity College Anti-Bullying Centre in Dublin, which was set up by Dr Mona O'Moore in the Education Department of Trinity College and was opened officially in January 1996.

It also offers a resource reference library open to the general public, advice and guidance, by phone or in person, and counselling services for both the victim and the bully.

With the help of his union and the Anti-Bullying centre, his case against Sligo County Council was brought to court. From that day onwards, Michael was assigned a different station officer from Liam O'Donnell, who was posted to another station in County Sligo.

He also visited a psychologist to help him come to terms with the years of abuse and learn ways to handle the feelings of anger and fear that would result from it.

Then, in July 2000, Michael was unexpectedly given an award – a bravery honour. Michael and his team of firefighters from Sligo fire station were given the citation of bravery for the role they played in a dangerous and dramatic rescue that saved the lives of two people.

Michael and his team were called to the scene of an accident in County Sligo, after a 35-tonne cement mixer overturned on a slope with a 4.5-metre (15-foot) incline. Trapped underneath the vehicle was the driver of the mixer, Benny Cohen.

During the dramatic rescue, Subofficer David Garvey also became trapped under the vehicle and had to be rescued by his colleagues.

The new station officer from Sligo fire station paid tribute to his colleagues, who had risked their lives to drag the truck driver from danger.

'I am very proud of my crew. This award is for bravery beyond the call of duty and it's nice to be recognised for our efforts,' he said.

It was a scene very different from the previous year, when Michael was close to quitting his job at the fire station after suffering years of verbal abuse from his former boss. One of Michael's close friends said the heroic fireman felt 'vindicated' by the award after his compensation fight with Sligo Council.

'It was a difficult situation for Michael, and I know this award means an awful lot to him and his colleagues,' he said. 'I think this citation will be a vindication for him after he stood up against the bullying and intimidation he suffered for years.'

When an inquiry was eventually held in 2001 into the bullying, he broke down and cried in front of senior county council officials.

It took place at the High Court in Sligo and was attended by the county secretary, county engineer and an officer for SIPTU, the Services, Industrial, Professional and Technical Union, which represents more than 200,000 Irish workers from virtually every category of employment across almost every sector of the Irish economy.

'I fell apart at that meeting,' admits Michael. 'I begged – I admit it. I lost my voice. I wanted to go back to work.'

Senior counsel James Nugent, for Michael, said his client had been 'systematically abused, bullied and belittled' by a superior officer over an eight-year period. From evidence, he said, it also appeared that Michael had suffered to such an extent that he became suicidal at one stage.

Michael told the inquiry that the matter was investigated by the Anti-Bullying Centre at Dublin's Trinity College. The report by the centre found that he was 'subjected to frequent abuse and obscenities, aggression and threatening behaviour while constantly undermining his authority with criticism, false accusations, rumours and goading'.

Justice Paul Butler said the case brought about post-traumatic stress disorder.

The county council admitted liability and Justice Butler was asked to assess damages. He ordered Sligo County Council to pay £65,000 to Michael. The injury, he said, was his employers' fault.

Since the inquiry, Liam O'Donnell, has since retired and Michael is now station officer at Sligo fire station.

On awarding the damages, the judge described it as an unusual case.

He was wrong – it is not.

As in Michael's case, most bullying at work goes unrecognised. It is often put down to personality clashes and different management styles. This is why people are afraid to make a complaint, with men being especially reluctant to speak out. They feel complaining will make them look weak.

The answer, according to the Anti-Bullying Centre, is to stand up to your boss or whoever is bullying you.

'Don't be afraid that you will look weak. You'll become weak by allowing it to continue,' said a spokesman.

All organisations should realise that it happens,

and have systems in place to treat it sympathetically. Those who do the bullying need help as much as their victims.

The case of Michael just showed how even these hardened workers can be intimidated, traumatised and driven close to the brink by something many see as trivial but is very serious – bullying.

But, for now, Michael has turned his life around and put all those years of hurt and suffering behind him. He wants to concentrate on his family and all the precious time he lost while he was being bullied.

# 11

# Abbi Morrall, 15

**W**ith the sound of kids scurrying out of class for their mid-morning break, petite school-girl Abbi Morrall got up from her desk and picked up her neatly packed pencil case and notepad.

It was a typical November day at Westfield Junior School in Hinckley, Leicestershire. The sky was grey and rain drizzled lightly onto the large metal windows across the corridor.

As the sound of high-pitched voices became louder and louder, blonde Abbi walked out of her English class and made her way towards the canteen. She felt inside the pocket of her blazer and pulled out a one-pound coin – just enough for a chocolate bar and apple juice.

It wasn't unusual for Abbi to spend break time

on her own. Although she had a few friends at the school, she was more self-contained than the other kids. And she didn't see anything wrong with sitting on her own in the canteen while the other kids sat in groups.

As she walked down the narrow, tunnel-like hallway, brushing past the crowds of children opening up their lockers to get snack money, Abbi suddenly felt a tap on her shoulder.

'Oi, where you think you're going?' a girl's voice said behind her.

Abbi's heart sank. She recognised the voice: it was that of Sarah,* one of the girls who had been tormenting her for over four years.

'Don't think you're gonna be buying nothing,' Sarah said. 'Give me your money! Now!'

Abbi's heart started thumping loudly and her palms moistened. She knew exactly what awaited her if she didn't hand the money over.

'O-OK,' Abbi muttered nervously, as she gave the pound coin to Sarah.

'You really think you're something special, don't ya?' Sarah's voice drew closer, echoing in Abbi's ear. 'Well, you're not.'

Abbi could feel Sarah's hot breath on the side of her neck and a shiver ran down her spine.

*The name of the bully in this account has been changed.

'Please, leave me alone,' she thought, crossing her middle and forefinger. It was something she always did. 'Don't hurt me – don't hurt me,' she'd plead.

And with that, Sarah pulled away, letting out a sinister chuckle as she walked away with a gang of girls.

The experience left Abbi in a state of distress. She was petrified Sarah would come back for more. But she knew that, if she got to the canteen, Sarah wouldn't be able to touch her because there would be teachers everywhere to protect her.

Within seconds, Abbi reached the canteen's automatic doors and she sighed with relief. At least for now, she'd be safe.

Although the torment and name-calling was a regular occurrence, Abbi still felt terrified every time her bullies approached her.

It had all started in primary school in 1998. To this day, Abbi can't pinpoint exactly why the other children singled her out.

'I got on very well with the teachers and loved going to school,' Abbi says. 'Maybe they were jealous of me because I got good grades.'

Abbi wasn't like a normal six-year-old. She was more mature and spoke more eloquently than other kids her age. Her mother, Alison Faulkner, also noticed that her daughter was different from other girls her age. She wasn't interested in dolls and talking about makeup. She was more bookish and enjoyed learning about everything.

It just started as a few mean comments here and there. The girls in her class would call her 'skinny' and tell her she was a geek. But, within a few months, the comments got more vicious. On numerous occasions, she was thrown against the playground wall and threatened by a group of girls from the same year.

By the time she was nine years old, in Year Four, the bullying had spread through the whole school and Abbi was even being taunted by seven-year-olds in Year Two.

And the bullying wasn't restricted to just girls. Boys also verbally abused Abbi. At one point, Abbi felt the whole school was against her. Some days, the thought of killing herself even crossed her mind. Abbi wished the bullying would stop.

'I was getting hurt every single day and I felt the same thing every time: fear,' she says. 'Most of the time I felt scared because I didn't know what was going to happen the next day.'

Abbi felt alone. She was too scared to tell anyone in case her bullies found out and took revenge. She just couldn't understand why they'd picked her as a target.

'I felt very vulnerable, too,' she says. 'When I was with my friends, I was happy and bubbly, but, when I saw my bullies, I'd shrink in size and in personality.'

The bullying changed her life. Whereas before Abbi was resilient and outgoing, her bullies stole all her inner strength. Abbi's only escape from all the torment was when she got home and could be her usual self again.

Her parents never noticed their little girl changing. All they saw was the bubbly Abbi they knew and loved. There was no sign of the torment she was going through.

'I had to do this in a way if I wanted to keep it from my mum,' Abbi says.

Because Abbi was too scared to tell anyone, she kept it all bottled up for more than five years. 'Sometimes telling someone can be the hardest part,' she says.

In 2005, Abbi was threatened by another group of girls, who told her that a member of her family had been beaten up.

'You're next,' one of the girls said, looking Abbi straight in the eye. Abbi was very afraid.

'I've always said that words hurt more than actions,' she says. 'When you are hit, scars, bruises and wounds can be covered up or will eventually disappear. But words always stay in your head.'

## BEATING THE BULLIES

As the months went by, Abbi decided to talk to her headmaster about the bullying. She told him that other children in the school were stealing her break money and threatening to kill her.

Finally, one day in late 2002, Abbi was out on the school field at break time. A teacher spotted a group of girls from Abbi's year walk up to Abbi and start to throw punches at her. The girls took it in turns to strike Abbi as she cowered on the grass beneath them.

'Stop! Stop right now!' the teacher shouted, running towards the girls. He marched them straight to the headmaster's office and Abbi was told the situation would be resolved.

'We won't let them hurt you again,' the headmaster promised. Abbi believed them. But, within days, the bullying started all over again.

A few years later she was sent death threats by email from one of her bullies.

'You're gonna die, bitch!' it read.

Abbi realised that the bullying wasn't limited to the school playground. They could reach her at any time, in the confines of her home, too.

After five years of being verbally and physically abused, Abbi decided to stand up to her bullies. She knew she had to take action. She couldn't take the abuse any longer and realised the only way she could escape her bullies would be to change schools. But that meant telling her parents about the bullying.

One evening, Abbi sat her mum down in the kitchen and told her everything.

'Mum,' she whispered. 'Sit down.' Her hands were clammy and her whole body was shaking.

Abbi was terrified that her mum wouldn't believe her or would make her stay at that school.

'I need to talk to you,' she continued, fidgeting with her fingers. 'I want to change schools.' She started to cry. 'Everyone's bullying me. I'm so unhappy, Mum. I just don't understand why.'

As tears flooded down from Abbi's bright, blue eyes onto her porcelain skin, she looked so fragile. It broke her mum's heart. She sat transfixed for a few seconds. She couldn't believe how her precious daughter had been hiding this hurt for so many years.

She hugged Abbi tightly – more tightly than she'd ever done before.

'Don't worry. Me and your dad are here to help you,' she soothed in Abbi's ear. 'We won't let them hurt you any more.'

That was exactly what Abbi needed to hear.

When she bottled up her feelings, Abbi felt she couldn't cope. She wasn't sure how to deal with the pressure and what to say to the kids to make them stop hurting her.

Having told her mum, Abbi suddenly felt safe again. It was as though a huge weight had been lifted off her shoulders. She knew that nothing could hurt her because somebody else knew about it and would help.

In 2003, Abbi moved to another local school, Redmoor High in Hinckley.

But she was bullied there, too. But this time Abbi didn't want to suffer in silence for years, so she told her headteacher straightaway. The headmaster had a strong stance against bullying and put a stop to it.

As a result, Abbi then got involved in the school council. She also got involved in a peer-support scheme. This is a system set up for pupils at school to come and talk to other pupils of their own age about their problems.

It is all confidential, which means that it isn't mentioned unless it is something such as abuse at home.

In the school council, Abbi also got the chance to travel to the YMCA in Leicestershire and attend anti-bullying workshops. In these workshops, they got the chance to make their ideal bully and what they thought a bully looked like. They also performed drama about bullying.

She then became part of the Leicestershire Anti-Bullying Student Team (she's still working with them to help to reduce bullying in Leicestershire). It was then that she started to win awards. First was the Princess Diana Anti-Bullying Memorial Award, won by the Leicestershire team she was part of, and then an individual Champions of Respect award in 2003.

Maggie Turner, director of the Diana, Princess of Wales, Memorial Awards for Young People, said, 'We are absolutely delighted to present the first Diana, Princess of Wales, Anti-bullying Award to them. The dedication and hard work of this team resulted in a fall in bullying at both primary and secondary schools in the area, a remarkable achievement.'

Abbi used her £500 winnings, plus sponsorship money, to create a website offering help and advice to young bullying victims. Then her mum read about The Sharon Osbourne Show and decided to write in telling her about Abbi's website and past experiences.

'I told them about her, sent them an email. They were thrilled. They had a look at her website and said it was brilliant,' says Alison.

The Sharon Osbourne Show was launched in 2003 as a daily ITV offering featuring celebrity chat, music and interviews with special members of the public such as Abbi.

A few days later, Abbi got a reply saying that they would like her to appear on the show. Abbi was overwhelmed with excitement. Thousands of people would be watching and it would be great publicity for her anti-bullying website.

Abbi said her TV interview touched on her past experiences of bullying.

'I was fine with it because, while I'm talking about my personal experiences, I know that somehow and some way it's helping somebody else, even if they just know that someone else is going through it,' says Abbi.

Sharon then arranged a dream day out for soccer-loving Abbi, which saw her interviewing the former England soccer captain David Beckham and training at his football academy.

Abbi is not only a fan but a footballer, one who has played for her school, Redmoor High, for three years and who hopes one day to become a coach.

Her day with Becks was one of the best of her life.

She then reappeared on the show a few days later, when her interview was broadcast.

'I had a great time on Monday recording the show. Sharon was lovely. All the media coverage has been a real boost for my website and it's become a full-time job answering all the questions and emails I receive,' she says.

'I can't believe the amount of media exposure I've received since appearing on the show, but it's helping to keep the site in the limelight and, hopefully, I can go on to help even more kids who're being bullied.'

Abbi's website had a massive surge of interest after the show, with more than eight thousand hits. The site also had more than thirty emails a day from young people experiencing bullying.

The workload of answering them surged so much that Abbi's mum, Alison Faulkner, has now given up her own job keeping accounts for her husband to help Abbi by going through the mail and answering the more common difficulties in line with Abbi's advice, which always involves telling someone who can help stop it.

Voluntary Action Hinckley and Bosworth is now helping the family to make the site a registered charity, which will help it to raise funds and expand.

'We exist to help people who are in established charities and people who want to set up charities. We have the knowledge, expertise and specialist skills to help,' says chief executive Greg Drozdz.

Since then, Abbi has appeared on BBC and ITV

news and in *Sunday* magazine, *Hello!* magazine, the *News of the World*, *Daily Star*, *Daily Mirror* and local newspapers such as the *Hinckley Times* and the *Leicester Mercury*. She has also appeared on BBC Radio Leicester and BBC Radio Nottingham.

Now, when Abbi looks back at her days of being bullied, she tries not to feel angry. Although she still has psychological scars from those days, she tries to focus on the positive.

'Throughout my experiences of bullying I was put up against a brick wall, threatened, called names, hit, picked on after school, left out of groups, sent threatening emails and many others,' she says. 'When you tell somebody it can turn your life around and it can change the person who you used to be.

'I have helped hundreds of people to cope and put a stop to their bullying because of my website,' she says.

Abbi feels sorry for the bullies. 'They are the people with a problem, not me,' she says. 'They also need help.'

Abbi's website can be found at: www.abs-kids.co.uk

# Mhairi Walker, 18

Sitting in the living room at their home in Stirlingshire, in Scotland, fifteen-year-old Mhairi Walker's family were entranced by their young daughter playing the saxophone.

As her light-brown hair draped across her small, round shoulders, Mhairi looked angelic.

It was a typical Sunday afternoon in the Walker household. During the week, Lynn and Andrew Walker worked hard. Lynn had dedicated years to helping youngsters deemed to be society's most disruptive children.

She held art classes for violent pupils at Falkirk Council as part of its social-inclusion policy aimed at keeping bullies in mainstream education. She was also in the process of setting up her own arts business.

Andrew Walker worked as a senior design manager for a construction firm.

They were both extremely demanding jobs. So the couple liked nothing better than to spend time with their children at weekends.

Growing up in Scotland, Mhairi was a shy and sensitive child. She did not have many friends at school and was deemed a loner by most of her peers. But she was a talented girl.

Ever since she can remember, she had been passionate about learning the saxophone. Now, at the age of fifteen, she had finally fulfilled her ambition to be an accomplished musician.

On 31 August 2004, Mhairi went to school* as normal. Lunchtime was the same as every other day. She sat alone in the crowded canteen and tried hard to blend in. There was always an empty space on each side of her.

With her shoulders hunched and eyes closely fixed to the plate in front of her, she shovelled the food down as fast as possible.

But on this particular day, Mhairi did not go unnoticed. Another pupil, a girl from the year above Mhairi, spotted the fear in Mhairi's eyes.

*The school in this case study cannot be named for legal reasons.

Sensing the schoolgirl's vulnerability, she headed straight for Mhairi. She crept up right behind her.

'You fat cow!' the girl shouted in Mhairi's ear, as she took a mouthful of food. The girl then grabbed a clump of Mhairi's thick, brown hair and dragged her from her seat. As a terrified Mhairi fell to the ground, the girl kicked her head against the hard floor.

Woozy and disoriented, Mhairi could not muster the strength to stand up. As the girl looked down at her, she sniggered.

'This'll show you,' she said, kicking Mhairi with all her force.

She then started to punch Mhairi and stamp on her neck, in full view of hundreds of other pupils. It was a random, unprovoked act of savage violence.

When the girl eventually ran out of steam, Mhairi lay on the floor in agony. With blood pouring from her nose and mouth, she was unable to move. There was even a footprint on Mhairi's arm from where the girl had stamped on her.

Teachers scrambled to the scene. The headmaster phoned Mhairi's mother, Lynn, immediately.

'Your daughter's been beaten up,' a teacher told Lynn. 'But we can't phone the police – only parents can lodge a complaint.'

Lynn was so distressed that she did not take in

what the teacher said. She jumped into her car and drove round to the school.

'My poor baby,' she cried out when she saw Mhairi lying on the nurse's bed covered head-to-toe in blood, falling in and out of consciousness.

With the help of a teacher and a male pupil, Lynn carried her daughter to the car and rushed to the nearest hospital. Mhairi was given a series of X-rays, while her mother alerted the rest of her family to the day's events.

'She's been badly bruised,' medical staff later told Lynn. 'But she's going to be OK.'

The next day, Mhairi was released from hospital. With the sense of shock and confusion now subsiding, Lynn mulled over what Mhairi's teacher had told her: that the school could not phone the police – only parents could.

'What kind of appalling policy is that?' she asked her husband, Ian.

They contacted the police to lodge a complaint. The case was referred to the Scottish Children's Reporter Administration (SCRA), which is the national body responsible for providing a world-class care and justice system for all Scotland's children.

Meanwhile, Mhairi's parents were fuming at the way their daughter had been treated by her school.

After the attack, Lynn wanted to go public and spoke out to the media.

'My beautiful, talented fifteen-year-old girl has been the victim of a terrible bullying attack at school,' she said. 'It has quite simply turned her life upside down.'

Meanwhile, Mhairi's bully was excluded from school for five days. Mhairi, on the other hand, was too frightened to return to school fearing a repeat of the incident. Instead, with her Standard Grade mock exams looming, Mhairi was forced to study at home.

This was a particularly big blow because Mhairi had been on course to get top marks in her Standard Grades, the Scottish equivalent of GCSEs.

'Although this girl is entitled to have school work sent home while she was excluded, Mhairi apparently has no such right,' said Lynn. 'Work is sent only because her teachers, who have been extremely helpful and supportive, volunteered to arrange it.'

Three months after the attack, Mhairi was still suffering pains in her back and was too scared to return to school.

'She's studying at home, but it's ridiculous because she doesn't have access to the things she needs,' said Lynn at the time. 'It's beyond belief that my daughter, who's done nothing wrong, is being treated like this while the bully gets away with it.'

The situation had a profound effect on the whole family.

'Our lives have changed because we're being forced to consider options we previously would've dismissed, such as private education,' said Lynn.

'I have felt at times like leaving Scotland because of this horrendous experience, but it's my country and this is my town. Why should we have to leave?'

Then, in 2005, Mhairi was told by the school that she could return if she sat alone during break times – to limit the risk of a further attack and avoid her bully on her way to classes. Different routes to classes would also be devised, ensuring the girls' paths do not cross.

But Mhairi and her family were enraged.

'I want the education minister to do something about this because it is so unfair,' Mhairi told the media.

Lynn was also devastated by this new development. 'I enjoyed working with troubled children in the past but I'm angry because the children who cause all the trouble are given special care while the kids who behave are punished,' said Lynn.

'I've gone home many nights with a deep sense of satisfaction and pride that I have in my own small way made a difference to their lives by instilling much-needed self-esteem.'

But her deep-rooted belief in social inclusion in schools has now been shattered by the horrific ordeal experienced by her own daughter and the devastating effect it has had on their entire family.

'That's why I now believe the system I've supported so passionately is effectively a sham,' Lynn added.

Around that time, it also emerged that the bully would only have to visit a social worker for 'voluntary advice and guidance' as part of her punishment.

'The bully's getting all the special treatment while I have to stay at home and risk my exam results. Why do bullies have all the rights?' Mhairi told the press.

A report was then released by the government stating that Scotland's schools were excluding one child every two minutes as head teachers battled growing classroom anarchy.

'The shocking state of indiscipline in our schools is now more obvious than ever. Temporary exclusion does not necessarily deter the excluded child or others,' Lord James Douglas-Hamilton, education spokesman for the Scottish Tories, said at the time.

## BEATING THE BULLIES

The Scottish National Party also spoke out about the issue of exclusion in schools.

'Exclusion should act as a deterrent and hopefully we will see the figures reduce as disruptive pupils realise head teachers will act harshly,' Scottish National Party education spokeswoman Fiona Hyslop said.

'We keep hearing about the Scottish Executive's new powers for headteachers to permanently exclude pupils – why hasn't that happened in this case? Why is a hardworking, decent girl like Mhairi being punished like this?' she added.

Julia Swan, director of education at Falkirk Council, said council bosses had 'listened very carefully to the family's concerns and have investigated them fully'.

'Following extensive discussions with the family, arrangements have been put in place to allow Mhairi to return to school,' she added. 'We will continue to work with the family to resolve this matter in Mhairi's best interests.'

But the council ruled out all possibility of the bully being excluded because of the likelihood that she would appeal successfully.

A spokesman for the Scottish Children's Reporter Administration said it was unable to comment on specific cases. 'We are concerned for the welfare of all children and young people who come to our attention, whether as the victim or the perpetrator,' he added.

The Executive spokeswoman, too, said officials could not comment on Mhairi Walker's case. 'Bullying is unacceptable and must be tackled wherever it arises. We have also given the power to exclude pupils permanently back to headteachers, but it is for them and not us to decide when that is appropriate,' she said.

But Lynn was still fuming. 'Many simply cannot believe this bully has been allowed to stay at the school, because my daughter is not the only person to suffer at her hands,' she said. 'We don't want punishment for punishment's sake. We want this child to be shown that the way she's acted is totally unacceptable. But this is something "voluntary" advice and guidance and a quiet chat with a social worker is unlikely to provide.'

As a result of the attack, Mhairi was exposed to a world where the need for personal responsibility had simply disappeared.

'One of the saddest aspects of this incredible saga is that my daughter – a bright, pretty teenager who was so full of confidence and life – has lost respect for authority,' said Lynn.

Like most families, the Walkers wanted only the

best for their children and tried to instil into Mhairi the need for respect and trust in authority.

'But she's understandably reluctant to place much faith in an education authority that's failed her on every level,' added Lynn. 'We also taught them that, for every right, there is a responsibility.'

But the fact that Mhairi had the courage to speak out about her ordeal is testament to her refusal to give in and to allow this situation to get the better of her.

As the she tried to pick up the pieces of her life again, Mhairi made the bold move of returning to her school. She wanted to face her demons.

In late 2005, Mhairi walked back inside the school canteen where she had been savagely attacked.

The reason for the visit was a Children in Need charity event to raise awareness for bully victims. It took a great deal of courage to venture into a place she previously loved so much, but she did.

But the day proved very emotional for Mhairi. 'All the memories from my attack came flooding back,' she says.

That evening, when Mhairi returned home exhausted, she burst into tears. She poured out all her thoughts and fears, allowing the torment of the previous few years to spill out.

For now, Mhairi believes everyone should be

determined to stand up to bullies. She is also calling for the government to do more about the issue.

'If we can do it, surely our ministers and education bosses can also find the courage,' she says.

Lynn was equally determined. 'I'm confident we're not alone and that throughout Scotland there are other children in a similar position who are being bullied.

'I hope they've been given extra confidence by our story because, despite our suffering, we will not give in,' she added.

# 13

# Amy Evans, 16

As pretty Amy Evans bounded down the stairs at her house in Swindon, a large town located in Wiltshire in the southwest of England, her parents beamed with delight.

It was not long ago that their daughter had been suffering from severe depression and was on the brink of a nervous breakdown. Just two years before, fourteen-year-old Amy's idyllic life was about to be turned upside down.

'Look at that geek over there!' a girl from Dorcan Technology College shouted outside the school gates. It was June 2005.

A gang of six were pointing and laughing at Amy's eleven-year-old brother Matthew as he made his way home that afternoon. They watched him cross over the street to avoid them and followed him. Within minutes, they had circled Matthew.

'Let's have some fun with him!' a boy laughed, nudging Matthew's shoulder.

Matthew was terrified.

'Nah,' replied one of the girls. 'Let's just play with him first.'

As they carried on teasing Matthew, his older sister Amy walked out of classes and made her way out of the school gates. Within seconds, she noticed the group lunge at her brother. She ran as fast as she could towards them. But, as she got closer, she saw one of the boys punch Matthew in the face.

Matthew immediately fell to the floor and lay helpless as his sister watched the boys and girls kick him repeatedly.

'Stop!' she cried out. 'Leave him alone!'

But the gang just kept striking him.

'I was scared he was going to be killed,' Amy recalls.

As she approached the scene, one of the boys dragged Matthew off the floor and head-butted him. Amy screamed at them to leave him alone. This time, they listened.

Once they left the scene, Amy picked her brother off the floor and carried him inside the school.

She immediately told her headmaster, who

phoned for an ambulance. Although Matthew had only superficial injuries such as cuts and bruises, he could have been killed in that incident.

Amy's parents were fuming. They could not understand how these children had been allowed to attack their son in broad daylight.

But the headmaster at Dorcan College assured them he would try to find out who attacked their son and take action.

The next day, the gang of bullies found out that Amy had told the headmaster, and turned their attention on her. They wanted vengeance. For the next few weeks, Amy endured relentless taunts by the gang.

'You made a big mistake,' said one of the girls. 'Now you're going to pay for telling tales.'

One particular day, in late June, Amy was walking home from her local corner shop when the gang, who all lived nearby, approached her.

They began shouting abuse at her and throwing gravel from the ground. Then, out of the blue, one of the girls walked straight up to Amy and spat in her face. It was a degrading and savage act. Wiping the spit off her face, Amy was mortified. She cried all the way back home.

Just one week later, Amy felt she could not cope any longer. 'I was all alone,' she says. 'I was too embarrassed to tell my parents or friends in case they thought I was exaggerating.'

Instead, she went into her parents' medicine cabinet and reached for a packet of paracetamol. That night, as the rest of the family slept peacefully, Amy lay in her bed sobbing. She reached for the packet of pills and stuffed as many as she could inside her mouth. Within minutes, the pills had taken effect.

Meanwhile, her brother Matthew could not sleep and knocked on his sister's door for company. He waited a few seconds but there was no response.

'Amy?' he whispered. 'It's me! Can I come in?'

But there was still no answer.

Pushing the door open, he found his sister draped on her bed, with an empty medicine packet in her hand.

'Mum!' he shouted. 'It's Amy!'

Her parents jolted out of bed and ran into her room. What they saw shocked them to the core. Their beautiful, innocent daughter had tried to kill herself.

They rushed her to hospital, where she had her stomach pumped.

'That image will haunt our family for ever,' her parents say. 'I would not wish it on any parent.'

When Amy was released the next day, she was in

a state of shock. Her parents informed the school and demanded more action be taken against their daughter's tormentors.

Meanwhile, Amy recovered at home and was allowed back to school for half-day lessons.

Despite surviving the first attempt on her life and seeing a counsellor, Amy still could not face the thought of being bullied again.

The final straw came when, just one week later, the gang threatened to pour yoghurt over Amy. After a week of being taunted with shouts of 'overdose girl', Amy could not face life any longer. So, on 24 June, she asked a friend to buy her a packet of paracetamol from the local chemist. She swallowed fourteen tablets, on top of the two painkillers she had already taken for a headache on the bus home.

It was a potentially lethal cocktail.

Her mother, Rachel, was at home at the time and found Amy within seconds. She rushed her daughter to hospital again. Amy was lucky to be alive. The dose of paracetamol she had taken would have killed her if her mother had not found her so quickly.

'It was the bullying that made me do it,' says Amy. 'I just wanted to scare them so they would think about what they were doing.'

It was a cry for help.

'It's awful,' said her mother Rachel. 'I was terrified I was going to lose my daughter.'

Amy's parents informed the police and her college. Wiltshire police confirmed they had received a complaint from the family and were investigating.

'Fortunately,' said Rachel, 'the police have now been involved and have the names of the bullies, so we hope they're made to care in the very near future. We sincerely hope they're arrested and hauled off by police for questioning. We'd like to think they'll be charged and brought before a court, but at the very least they should be shamed and shunned.'

Dorcan Technology College also released a statement. 'We take bullying allegations very seriously,' said a college official at the time. 'But it is our policy not to discuss individual cases, so it would not be appropriate for us to comment further.'

While police investigated the incident over the next few weeks, Amy spoke to the media.

'I've never thought about suicide before,' she said. 'It was so horrible that I'm now 99 per cent sure I would never try it again.'

Her mother Rachel was devastated. 'It's awful. Her life is fine except for the bullies,' she said. 'She's just a typical teenage girl with lots of friends. I'm totally emotionally exhausted by all of this, but I have to be strong for the children.'

Rachel also refused to send her daughter back to Dorcan Technology College.

'Enough is enough,' she said at the time. 'I'm not going to send Amy back to the lions' den'.

The school bullies were hounding her every day, often as she made her way home from school, so Rachel decided the only option was to keep her away. Instead, she schooled her at home.

Six months later, Amy was given a place at the Riverside Centre, a special school for vulnerable youngsters.

'Of course, the bullies don't see themselves as evil, and they are probably not perceived that way by their teachers and their circle of friends,' Rachel now says. 'They may well bring reasonable reports home, get good exam grades, or represent their school at sport.

'But the gang member who told Amy to kill herself was as guilty of a criminal offence as those thugs who go out to mug grannies for their pensions.'

Amy is a lot happier at Riverside – away from her tormentors.

'I was nervous about starting at the Riverside

because the last time I was at school it was horrible,' said Amy.

Amy kept quiet for the first few days of starting at Riverside. But she need not have worried because, within weeks, she had made lots of friends and loved her new school.

'The best thing is my grades have gone up loads,' she said. 'When I was in mainstream school I was only getting Ds but I had a mock GCSE English exam the other day and I got a B, and I've got a B for my English coursework as well.'

Amy also preferred the smaller class sizes.

'Riverside is much smaller, with only thirty-six pupils, and everyone's been through problems so everyone understands how you feel,' said Amy. 'We all look out for each other.'

Amy's family even took the drastic decision to move from their home in Liden to the other side of town – just to give Amy the new start she was longing for.

'Riverside is absolutely brilliant – she's achieved a lot there,' said Rachel. 'It's been a good outcome and much better than keeping her in mainstream education. Now she'll have to go out into the big bad world, but she has the confidence to deal with it.'

The Riverside Centre undoubtedly turned Amy's

life around. She is now studying A-levels in English, psychology and sociology and wants to become a counsellor or youth worker to help teenagers.

And she has a simple message for anyone else who might be being bullied right now: 'Go and get help because, if you don't do anything, the bullying won't stop.'

And her mother Rachel echoed that advice: 'We were living in hell. It was a nightmare while Amy was being bullied and we didn't know what was going to happen to her, but there really is light at the end of the tunnel.

'I kept on at the education authority to get her a place at the Riverside and when she got that I wanted to move because the bullies were local kids. When we loaded our stuff onto the removal lorry I was so happy. Now I'm not on edge all the time when Amy goes out.'

And Rachel says the whole family is happier now.

'Matthew was really badly affected by what had happened to Amy and was even targeted by the same kids, but now he's doing really well and we're all happy,' says Rachel.

Just two years ago, Amy Evans did not think her life could get any worse. But, in the twelve months after she changed schools, her life was transformed.

Brave Amy took the most positive step she

possibly could to stand up to the bullies who made her life a living hell. She spoke to the media and allowed her photo and her terrifying story to be used to warn others of the effects these evil schoolchildren have.

'Two years ago I thought I wouldn't be able to carry on because of the bullies, but now everything has changed and I'm really happy,' said Amy.

'Amy's strength and courage has shown her tormentors for what they really are: weak, cowardly and inadequate bullies to be despised,' added her mother.

She rarely thinks about the torture she endured at the hands of bullies in 2005.

'I try not to think of those times now,' Amy said. 'I was really scared. I wouldn't leave the house and wouldn't go to school for six months. Now I feel much better and go out every day. I've moved on and got on with my life.'

And Amy has urged other children to speak out if they are being bullied and not to feel ashamed.

'They should tell a teacher and their parents when it happens and write it down,' she says. 'Anyone can beat the bullies, just like I did.'

# 14

# Jacqui Gill, 45

'**H**ey! Look at her!' a group of girls sneered, pointing at eight-year-old Jacqui Gill running round the sports field. 'She's so fat she can't run!'

It was school PE lesson and Jacqui was the brunt of all the jokes yet again.

'It was always the same,' she says.

Every PE lesson the captains picked teams and she was always the last girl standing. Among all the slender young girls, Jacqui stuck out like a sore thumb. She was a size 12 and only four foot three. It was not easy for a girl like Jacqui. She was desperately lonely and, with not a single friend, she found that food was becoming her only comfort.

The bigger Jacqui got, the more she hated sport

and started making excuses to miss lessons. It did not help that she had bright red hair. Stout and round, she reached a size 16 by her teens.

'Oi, Duracell battery!' her classmates would call out to her as she walked by in the playground. The nickname implied she was short and orange.

The bullying was amplified because Jacqui was such a shy child.

'I just couldn't seem to talk to the other kids,' Jacqui admits.

Despite the extent of the bullying, Jacqui never felt confident enough to fight back against her bullies. By that time, she was too ashamed of herself.

'There was a part of me that felt I deserved the abuse,' she says.

During the next few years, she tried desperately to slim down. But every attempt she made to give up excess food would result in her binge-eating.

'Food was my friend,' she says. 'Without it, I was desperately lonely.'

At the age of sixteen, she weighed about 89 kilos (14 stone, or 196 pounds) and had struggled with her weight for over ten years.

When she left school in 1970, she met and married Peter, an admin official in the Royal Air Force, and the couple moved into a family home in High Wycombe, Bucks.

'I did loads of faddy diets – like one where I just ate yoghurt for two weeks and ended up fainting. But I always put it all back on. On my wedding day I squeezed into a size 20 dress.'

They had two children, Anna and Jason, soon after. Jacqui was 114 kilos (18 stone, or 252 pounds) when she had her children.

'I had to have maternity clothes made for me. I felt too ashamed to go out to social functions that Pete and I were invited to,' she says.

But Jacqui was so scared of history repeating itself that she took extra care to feed her children a healthy diet.

'I didn't want them to be bullied, so I made sure they ate well,' she says.

But Jacqui just kept growing bigger and bigger.

By the time she was forty-one years old, she was carrying 133 kilos (21 stone, or 294 pounds) on her five-foot-seven frame and wore size 28 dresses.

Miserable and depressed, she would tuck into pizza and chips every night.

It was while taking her kids to school that Jacqui realised her obesity was getting out of control.

'It was only a short walk but I'd be out of breath by the time we got to the school gates. The kids would moan that I was walking too slowly,' she says.

## BEATING THE BULLIES

It was also around that time that the family bought Anna a pony, called Pepsi, for her tenth birthday. Jacqui asked the vet how much Pepsi could carry.

'About fourteen stone,' the vet replied.

But, when the stable owner looked at Jacqui and then shot a glance at Pepsi, she laughed.

'Poor horse!' she cried out.

After the stable owner's remark, Jacqui was distraught. Over the next few weeks, Peter and their two children went out for long walks with Pepsi; Jacqui would stay at home.

Only a few steps would make Jacqui out of breath at this point. Even walking to the stables with Anna was hard. But, inside, Jacqui was seething with envy. She also felt she was losing the best years of her children's lives.

'I wanted to ride Pepsi and spend time with my kids,' she says. 'But it was impossible: I would have crushed Pepsi.'

A few months later, she decided to take decisive action.

'At first, I didn't tell anyone when I joined my local slimming club,' she says. 'I didn't want to be a failure again.'

Jacqui, who was still wearing size 28 clothes, feared she would fail to diet if she knew how much she had to lose. So she asked her slimming club leader to take a note of her starting weight and keep it in a sealed envelope.

This time, Jacqui was kept motivated by the memories of those sports lessons and seeing her daughter Anna ride Pepsi.

She ditched the junk food once and for all.

'I was determined to succeed. I lost four pounds in the first week. Suddenly I was eating fruit and vegetables when before I'd snack on crisps,' she says.

After ten months on the diet, she reached 82 kilos (13 stone, or 182 pounds) and was light enough to ride Pepsi. That day, she climbed up on Pepsi and she trotted off, with her two children watching.

'I felt like a little girl again as I trotted around the field on her for the first time,' she said. 'Seeing Anna so proud of me was wonderful.'

Jacqui had found a new sense of self-worth. In July 2005, she reached her target weight of about 69 kilos (10 stone 12 pounds, or 152 pounds).

'After stepping off the scales and seeing I'd lost ten stone, the leader opened the envelope. I couldn't believe I was more than twenty stone when I first started,' she says.

'I would never have tried to lose that weight if I had known my real size,' she says.

The first thing she bought herself was a size 12

pair of jodhpurs. She still goes riding five or six times a week.

'I now compete in local show-jumping competitions. And, when I walk the children to school, they now tell me off for walking too quickly for them! I've even won rosettes for show jumping – not bad for the girl who was too fat for PE,' she says.

Thirty years later, she had proved everyone wrong.

Pete was even more thrilled when his wife lost weight, since it meant Jacqui finally agreed to go to his annual work summer ball for the first time ever.

'I wanted to be slim and glamorous when I made my debut in front of his workmates,' she says.

When the invitation to the ball landed on the doormat, she rushed out and bought a dark-red dress in a slinky size 12.

'I felt amazing. Pete was so proud of me,' she said. 'If we hadn't bought Anna a pony I'd probably still be fat, so I've a lot to thank Pepsi for.

'I feel like a new woman and I still can't help smiling when I slip into my jodhpurs every morning.'

# 15

# Georgia Foster, 41

**B**rushing past crowds of people on the busy streets of Piccadilly Circus in Central London last year, brunette Georgia Foster was on her way to a ten-year reunion with colleagues from her job as a secretary in a prestigious investment bank in the City of London.

   She looked forward to an evening of catching up with old friends and reminiscing about the past. As the night wore on, more and more champagne flowed and the group became increasingly rowdy.

   Perched on the bar taking a sip from her glass of wine, Georgia locked eyes with a former boyfriend, an investment banker she had worked closely alongside ten years prior.

Their relationship lasted only a few months but Georgia was mortified when he ended it with no explanation.

He smiled at Georgia and walked towards her.

'Wow, you've really come a long way,' he leaned in and whispered softly in her ear.

She felt a tingle run down her spine. The chemistry between them was still evident.

'Thank you,' she replied coyly, brushing a piece of her auburn hair away from her face.

'You know we had a nickname for you at the office?' he chuckled.

Georgia was bemused. She had been aware that the group of bankers had derogatory names for some of the other secretaries – but not her.

'I'm not sure I should tell you,' he said.

'No, go on,' Georgia insisted. 'It's in the past now.'

He leant back and took a large gulp of his bottle of beer.

'Are you sure?' he checked one last time.

'Yes!' Georgia screeched.

'We called you the Fat Ozzie,' he told her.

Georgia was devastated. In that one moment, her confidence was utterly shattered.

'Oh, um…' she muttered. 'It's a good thing I've lost weight then?'

Humiliated and embarrassed, Georgia got up from her stool and made her excuses to leave.

When she moved to London in the summer of 1996, Georgia had endured more than twenty years of being bullied for her size. She had got used to using humour to distract from hurtful comments about her weight.

It all started when she was growing up in Melbourne, Australia. When she reached puberty at 13 years old and started to develop a more womanly figure, the other girls from her class at Strathcona private girls' school began to tease her.

'Hey, Fatso!' the girls would shout out from across the playground as she walked in to school.

Never a day went by without her being verbally abused about her large frame. Georgia remembers one particularly upsetting incident. It was Sports Day at school and Georgia was nervous about running in front of her classmates.

She was only 14 years old but she already weighed over 14 stone.

'Right,' she told herself. 'You can do this.'

As the whistle blew, Georgia began to run.

She had only been running for a few seconds when one of the other girls turned to her and shouted:

'You'll never make it to the end, Wobbly Knees!'

Georgia's eyes filled up with tears. Despite the

physical pain she was in, her mental upset was far greater.

She gave up on the race and hobbled to the sidelines, her head bowed in defeat.

'Why can't I be thin like the other girls?' she asked her mother, Beverley, that night over dinner.

'Oh darling,' she soothed. 'It's just a bit of puppy fat.'

But growing up in Australia, where there is a large Greek population of more than 600,000, Georgia was often referred to as the 'fat, Greek girl' because of her dark, curly hair.

Her parents, Beverley and Richard, and older sister Virginia being slim made matters even worse for Georgia. As she grew into a grumpy overweight teenager, she never felt like she fitted in.

Her classmates would relentlessly tease her about her weight – which just made Georgia eat even more.

She was in a vicious cycle.

One particularly cruel girl at her school would regularly write 'Fat Ass' on a piece of paper, scrunch it up and throw it at Georgia from across the classroom.

Children were not the only ones to pick on her.

'Oh, you used to be such a lovely, little girl. What happened to you?' one of Georgia's teachers even said to her once, referring to Georgia's size. Georgia was just 15 years old, but those words stuck in her mind.

Her family never put her on a diet but Georgia's inner critic told her she was fat and ugly. So she just kept eating and eating. She would binge on cereal, toast, sandwiches, biscuits, cakes and sweets every day.

'I realised body image was important and as I was naturally shy, I started to overeat and I hid behind my weight,' Georgia says now.

Over and over, Georgia tried all sorts of fad diets. And at the age of 16, she met her first boyfriend. He was a year older and called Christopher*.

But all was not perfect.

Before meeting him, she had successfully managed to drop six dress sizes in under six months and was down to a petite size eight. But during the course of their relationship, Georgia began to feel insecure and anxious.

He sensed her vulnerability and would often call her offensive names.

'He undermined me constantly,' she says now.

Her best friend Fiona at the time was a real beauty – she looked like Rachel Hunter – and Georgia always felt inadequate next to her. She saw herself as the 'dumpy friend'.

'Looking back on my past, I realised that going through my teenage years I started to attract negative

*Name has been changed.

relationships and bullying boyfriends because of my low self-worth,' she says now.

As their relationship deteriorated, Georgia again turned to food for comfort.

Within months, she had piled back on all the weight she had lost and was back up to a size 14.

Christopher was repulsed by her weight gain and would repeatedly tell her that nobody else would have her because she was too overweight.

On one occasion, the couple went to stay in his family ski lodge in the mountains at Mount Bulla near Melbourne with friends.

One evening, the group were sitting round the fire at the lodge when Georgia, who was sat in a wooden chair, suddenly fell to the floor.

She had broken the chair.

'You fat cow!' Christopher shouted at her. 'You really need to go on a diet.'

Georgia was mortified. That night, she confronted him.

'Why are you so nasty?' she asked him.

'You've got fat,' he told her matter-of-factly. 'Are you going to do something about it?'

Georgia was desperate to please him. 'I'll try,' she pleaded with him. But the truth was that the pressure just made her want to eat more.

The final straw came when one night, his mother

told Christopher he would be better off with Georgia's 'thinner, more beautiful' best friend, Fiona.

Just a few weeks later, the couple broke up after two years together.

Georgia decided it was time she tried to make something of her life. She enrolled on a secretarial course at a college in Melbourne.

Away from her old friends, Georgia wanted to make a fresh start.

She was at her heaviest in years, weighing 68 kilos. Faced by this, she went on a healthy eating plan and lost two stone and by the end of her course, one year later, Georgia was back down to a size 10.

At the age of 18 in 1984, she went to work for her father's family business Music Maker – a company which built sound systems for shops.

Georgia worked as their Office Manager, doing all the accounts and paper work. During this time she had a few short relationships, but it wasn't until a year later that she met Mark*, who was a few years older, through friends.

She was struck by his sharp humour and quick mind. Mark loved her curves.

Within a year, they had moved into a rented house together – but soon after he was fired from

*Name has been changed.

his job as a Xerox sales person and was unemployed.

Mark stayed at home all day, becoming more and more depressed and resentful towards Georgia for having a job. He began to take his anger out on her.

'The only reason you've got a job is because your dad employed you,' he would tell her constantly.

Georgia had always been very close to her family and Mark was resentful of this because he did not have such close family ties.

'He was a very judgemental character and thought he was better than everyone,' says Georgia now.

He became increasingly angry and jealous as the months wore on. That is when he started to make derogatory comments about her body.

'You're such a lump,' he would tell Georgia.

Despite losing 14 kilos over the course of their relationship, Mark still continued to criticise her weight.

One evening, the couple hosted a dinner party at their home.

Georgia told them how her father was worried about her dramatic weight loss.

'You could still lose half a stone,' Mark quipped.

The table went silent.

Later that night, in bed, he blurted out, 'You're too fat to f**k.'

Georgia cried herself to sleep.

Eventually, Georgia's mother, Beverley paid for her daughter to take a two week holiday to Fiji in order to have some space to think about their relationship. On her return, Georgia went round to their house with a removal van and picked up her belongings.

She was finally putting an end to their destructive relationship.

Two years on, at the age of 26, Georgia had piled all the weight back on and was back up to a size 14.

She had seriously low self-esteem and ran away to a health farm called Camp Eden, just outside Melbourne, for two weeks to think about her future.

She had severe depression and even contemplated suicide. After numerous group therapy sessions, she returned home to her parents.

'I want to find myself and travel,' she told them.

She had come across a book at the health farm called *Embracing Ourselves* by Hal Sidra Stone, a psychologist in the USA.

Georgia enrolled on a course called Voice Dialogue run by the author at a college in California.

Four months later, she'd completed her course in the US and flew over to London in search of a new life, where she immediately enrolled on a well-known hypnotherapies course.

But she needed to supplement her income so she took up a job as a secretary in an investment bank. She remained a size 14 throughout her job there.

To deter from her feelings of inadequacy, Georgia became the office clown. She'd been binge-eating since she was 14 – but now it got worse.

She would have cereal, toast, flapjacks, and so on. But she says she was 'never brave enough' to be bulimic.

In the evenings, she would go out and drink a few bottle of wine with all her friends. At her biggest, she was 13 stone.

In 1996, Georgia finally qualified as a hypnotherapist. But by then she was 28 and stuck in a rut of dead-end relationships.

Finally, her luck turned when at the age of 33, Georgia met an Englishman called Derek* and remained in a stable relationship with him for three years.

He was very supportive of her and she reached her weight of 9 stone within a year of meeting him.

'The one thing you're not allowed to talk about is my weight,' she told him from the start.

He understood her past and treated her with respect. As a result, she was no longer in fear of food anymore. Her pride and sense of self-worth

*Name has been changed.

became more important, and she started to train herself to get away from her 'inner fat voice'.

Georgia qualified as a clinical hypnotherapist and inner voice dialogue trainer in 2001.

'I was given the gift to do what I do now,' she says.

All those children, all those boyfriends being cruel to her have made her the person she is now.

'A lot of people who bully are actually being bullied at home,' she added.

She now specialises in over-eating, over-drinking and self-esteem issues in her work as a clinical hypnotherapist.

She had finally beaten her bullies by losing weight and setting up a very successful hypnotherapy business. Ironically, Georgia also works with a number of investment banks and insurance companies as their in-house hypnotherapist.

'I thought I was not worthy to be loved,' she says. 'But now I know different.'

*Names of boyfriends have been changed.

# 16

# Maria Dixon, 40

Slumped on the sofa flicking through the satellite television channels at her home in Oldham, Manchester, in the north of England, Maria Dixon shot up in her seat.

'Have you ever wished you were thinner, had a smaller nose, whiter teeth?' asked a blurb. 'Here's your chance to make yourself perfect!'

The programme was called *Extreme Makeover* and anybody could apply to become a contestant.

As Maria fell back on the soft, plush cushions underneath her, she could not stop thinking about the programme.

Life had been one big roller-coaster ride for Maria and childhood bullying and violent relationships had taken their toll.

## BEATING THE BULLIES

When she was a youngster cruel classmates tormented her about her thick-rimmed glasses, crooked nose and wonky teeth.

Maria was also often the brunt of cruel playground taunts.

'I just hated school,' she says. 'I was bullied for my looks at school and the kids could be really nasty,' she says. 'The final straw came at the age of seventeen, when a group of girls attacked me in the shopping mall.'

Maria was on her way to the cinema with a friend when four girls approached her and grabbed her purse. Before Maria had the chance to scream, the girls had fled through the fire escape.

'I didn't phone the police,' she says. 'There was no point because I knew the girls would deny it.'

Instead, she decided to leave school altogether. The bullying had affected her so badly that Maria was unable even to contemplate returning to education.

'I hated everything about myself at the time,' she said. 'I just wanted to crawl under a stone and disappear.'

Maria's low opinion of herself worsened when she met her first boyfriend at the age of eighteen.

'He was arrogant,' she says. 'He thought he was above me.'

One night, during a ferocious row between the pair, her boyfriend slapped her in the face.

'I forgave him,' she says. 'Because I was so insecure and thought I didn't deserve to be loved.'

But, when she discovered he had been having an affair with a work colleague, Maria dumped him.

It was not long before another man subjected Maria to mental abuse. Her second boyfriend made constant derogatory comments about her teeth and wavy hair.

'He never hit me, but his words could be so nasty that he didn't need to,' says Maria.

She split with her first husband when she was pregnant with her second child, Danielle, now twenty.

'I was sure I was facing a lifetime alone, because no man could want to be with me,' she says.

Maria says 'I thought I was too ugly to love,' she says.

Having sworn off men for good, Maria finally found true love with David, aged forty-two, in 1995.

'David treated me with love and respect from the very beginning,' she said.

They married in 2001, although Maria was still unable to put the past traumas behind her.

'Even though I was in a happy relationship, I still

had issues with my appearance,' she said. 'Every time I looked in the mirror I saw all of the negative parts of my past. I couldn't escape it. I wanted to look different, especially my crooked teeth.'

So, after discussing the subject with David, Maria decided to have cosmetic surgery. She just desperately wanted a makeover so she could start feeling positive about life and her looks again.

'It wasn't a weight thing, as I was used to going to the gym and felt quite healthy – I just wanted my curves back in all the right places,' she says.

Maria could not afford to have the surgery she wanted so she applied to feature on Living TV's Extreme Makeover in order to get it done for nothing. But she was terrified because it would mean six weeks of surgery.

Egged on by her husband, she took the plunge and applied to the programme. Just a few weeks later, she received a phone call from the television company saying she had been selected.

'You've got a lot of work ahead of you,' the producer joked.

But Maria was ecstatic. Her dreams were finally coming true. She had liposuction to go from a size 14 to a size 12, a brow lift, eyelid lift and a thread lift to her cheeks.

Maria also had her eyes lasered to correct her

vision, and in addition underwent extensive dental work.

Her dental work cost £14,000; a lift to face/forehead cost £3,000. The laser eye surgery cost £4,200; her liposuction to stomach, thighs and chin cost £7,500. Then there was her nose job costing £4,000, and her eyelid reduction £2,800. She was thrilled with the results.

'I love my new look. I feel like a new person,' she said. 'I had to deal with a lot of internal issues, before I could even think about fixing the outside. I can't stop smiling.'

But she maintains that having cosmetic surgery was not a quick fix and not a decision she took lightly.

'I used to be shy and withdrawn,' she says. 'But now I'm strong and confident.'

But Maria's perfect new smile involved twelve hours of painful surgery.

'I had to be fed through a syringe for days, but it was so worth it,' she said. 'David couldn't speak at all at first, but when he realised it was still just me inside he was OK,' she laughed.

But now she could not be happier.

Her newfound confidence has meant that she is already rising more quickly in her career and she has finally been able to lay her inner demons to rest.

**BEATING THE BULLIES**

'Having cosmetic surgery is not a decision I took lightly,' she says. 'I feel so pleased with my new look and I can't stop smiling.

'It was so worth it,' she said. 'The first time I saw my smile in the mirror I cried with happiness. I'm so pleased with the final result. I can't explain how it has changed my life – it's amazing.'

After her transformation was complete, Maria Dixon finally got the look of her dreams.

# 17

# Abigail Worth, 18

**W**alking down the corridor at school, Abigail Worth could see the other girls from her class whispering.

'She looks so weird!' hissed one, pointing at Abigail.

Abigail sighed and walked on. After years of being teased, she was used to it. She knew exactly what they were laughing at – her face.

'Growing up, I didn't realise that I was different from the other kids,' she says. 'But they did.'

At primary school in Lincoln, in eastern England, people would stare at Abigail all the time.

'Here comes Popeye!' they would shout as she walked past.

They were referring to her eyes, which bulged out of her skull because of her flat face.

'It hurt,' says Abigail. 'But I got used to it.'

Fighting back the tears, she told herself that these children did not understand her condition. For Abigail suffered from Crouzon syndrome, a genetic disorder, and 50 per cent of the time it is passed on through the father's sperm. It causes the bones of the skull to fuse together. Pieces of the skull that have not fused are then pushed outwards to make room for the brain. This causes the distorted head and face shape.

'Two days after Abby was born I noticed her head was a funny shape,' says her mother Sally. 'But she was so cute, and I adored her.'

Before the age of four, Abby had to endure two operations at Great Ormond Street Hospital in London, England, to relieve pressure on her brain caused by her fused skull – leaving her with thirty stitches from ear to ear.

During her first operation, doctors removed a piece of bone from her forehead and cut it into pieces before inserting it into another part of her skull to give it a more normal shape. When doctors handed Abigail back to Sally her head was shaved and she had a line of stitches stretching across the top of it.

'The only problem was, I looked weird – I had no cheekbones and my face was flat,' says Abigail.

But, without these operations, she would have died. As she grew up, even adults talked down to Abigail. 'They thought I was stupid,' she says.

She was also very small, so people assumed she had Down's syndrome, a genetic disorder caused by the presence of all or part of an extra twenty-first chromosome. The condition is named after a British doctor, John Langdon Down, who described it in 1866.

It is characterised by a combination of major and minor differences in body structure, and can often be identified during pregnancy or at birth. It is associated with some impairment of physical growth and cognitive ability, and a distinctive facial appearance.

When Abigail turned seven years old in 1996, she went to a restaurant with her parents to celebrate. Sitting near them were a family with a son who was of a similar age to Abigail.

'Mummy, what's wrong with her face?' he cried out, pointing at Abigail.

He then started crying and screaming because he was frightened of the way Abigail looked. The boy's parents did nothing to diffuse the situation. Finally, Abigail also burst into tears.

'I felt like a freak,' she says. 'I was just devastated that I looked so terrible that I'd caused him to be upset.'

Abigail's family got up and left the restaurant straightaway without finishing their food. At that moment, Abigail realised she was very different from most children her age.

As she got older, she started to get used to the name-calling. Sometimes, she would even stand up to people.

One day, when Abigail was thirteen, a group of girls were staring at her at the bus stop near her school. They started laughing and pointing at her. But Abigail was enraged. She had had enough of the abuse and ignorance. She mustered all her courage and walked up to the girls to confront them.

'I know I'm gorgeous,' Abigail told them. 'But you don't have to stare!'

The girls looked on in shock and immediately stopped laughing. Putting a brave face on worked, but inside Abigail was hurt.

By the time Abigail was fourteen, the bullying had become unbearable.

'By then I looked like a mini-Frankenstein monster,' she says.

And the older she got, the more her face sagged and her eyes bulged.

'I just became more and more aware of how I looked,' she says. 'All my friends started dating boys, but no one even chatted me up.'

Now, not only were other children picking on her for having Crouzon syndrome, but they were also teasing her for being academic.

'In the end,' she says, 'I just stopped working hard at school so they'd leave me alone.'

It was not long before her mother noticed the change in her daughter. 'Is everything OK at school?' she asked Abigail one evening.

Abigail could not lie to her mother, so she told her everything: how the other children were bullying her and how she felt alone at her current school. Sally decided that her daughter should be removed from the school immediately.

Just a few weeks later, Abigail was offered a place at a new school in her area.

'Everyone was much nicer,' she says. 'But I still hated the way I looked.'

However, Abigail resigned herself to the fact that she would always look the way she did.

That same year, on her annual checkup with a specialist who dealt with her Crouzon syndrome, the doctor mentioned a new operation.

'We may be able to change the way you look,' he told Abigail.

She could not contain her eagerness. But because of the gravity of the operation involved, Abigail would have to wait until she turned sixteen.

'I had to wait a year,' she says. 'But I was so excited that I couldn't stop thinking about it!'

Around the same time, Abigail's parents came across a charity called Changing Faces, which helps people suffering with Crouzon syndrome, and made contact.

'It was brilliant,' says Abigail. 'For the first time I met other people in the same situation as me.'

Abigail was reassured to find out that she was not alone. But she was still desperate to have the operation to change her face.

On her sixteenth birthday, she was ready. In October 2004, she was admitted to Great Ormond Street Hospital in London. As she lay in bed, doctors explained they would peel the front of her face away from her skull, remove her forehead, extend her cheekbones and bring her top jaw forward.

The operation would take seven hours.

'It sounded terrifying,' says Abigail. 'But all I could think of was looking normal.'

Finally, Abigail would be able to wear sunglasses without them touching her eyeballs and she would be able to eat chewing gum because her teeth would fit.

As doctors wheeled the frightened Abigail into the operating theatre, she had butterflies.

'Good luck,' said her mother, clutching her daughter's hand one last time.

Abigail was given an anaesthetic and fell asleep within seconds.

Doctors then cut a 7.5-centimetre (3-inch) piece of bone from her skull, peeled her face back, removed her forehead bone, broke her jaw, and wired her head into a metal frame 15 centimetres (6 inches) wide.

Seven hours later, Abigail woke up again.

'I was confused,' she says. 'And in total agony.'

She had no idea where she was and was still drowsy from the anaesthetic.

'You look like you've been in a fight!' her mother laughed. Abigail had two black eyes and her face was puffy and bruised.

Over the next few months, Abigail had to endure wearing a metal frame to keep her face aligned.

'The doctors had to turn it every day to pull my facial bones forward,' she says. The next few weeks were agonising. 'It was the most painful thing that I've ever experienced in my life,' says Abigail.

'As she went into the last operation,' says Sally, 'she said, "I just want to look normal, Mum. Will I look normal after this?" I'd never heard her talk about wanting to be normal before – it broke my heart.'

Because her jaw had been broken, she could not chew or swallow properly, so Sally had to purée all Abigail's food. For two months, she lived on mashed potato, scrambled egg and ice cream.

'I really wanted the frame to come off, but I was so scared of what I would look like,' says Abigail.

It was also very uncomfortable to wear. Abigail could not sleep on her side and could not pull any clothes over her head, so she had to wear things that buttoned up the front or unzipped at the back.

The frame was finally taken off just before Christmas 2004, which involved another two-hour operation.

'I was really nervous about what I was going to look like because my face was still swollen when it was taken off,' she says. 'But after a week the swelling went down.'

That morning, she woke up and rushed to the mirror in her bathroom. She could not believe what she was seeing.

'I had cheekbones for the first time in my life!' says Abigail, who was overjoyed. 'I couldn't stop checking myself in the mirror,' she laughs.

Sally found it most difficult to get used to – she had been used to seeing Abigail for all those years looking totally different. But Abigail loved it straightaway. Finally, Abigail had the face she was meant to be born with.

She went back to school and nobody recognised her.

'I would pass friends in the corridors, and they would walk past me without saying anything' she says. 'I felt like a new girl who didn't know anyone!'

She is much more confident now as a result.

'I'm always out with my mates now,' she says. 'And I get loads of attention from boys now!'

Abigail is thrilled with her new face. And now she is a step closer to fulfilling her dream of becoming an actress. Her local theatre group put on a production of Peter Pan in 2006 to raise money for Great Ormond Street Hospital, and asked Abigail to take part.

'It was wonderful to step out on stage and feel confident in the way I looked,' she says. 'I'd never heard of or seen an actress who looked like me, with facial disfigurements, so it seemed like an impossible dream.'

Now Abby enjoys being the centre of attention – for the right reasons.

'I'm not dating, because I'm concentrating on my A-levels, but I go out much more than I used to,' she says.

It took two years for her face to settle down properly after the operation in order to make sure that all her bones had grown in the right place. But she had a scan at her local hospital in late 2006 and she was finally given the all-clear.

'My new face has given me the self-assurance that I've always longed for,' she says.

'I'm studying theatre studies for A-level and I just love being on stage.'

For now, Abigail does not need to have any more operations and can start pursuing her dreams.

Sally is also thrilled with her daughter's new face. 'She was always beautiful to me, but now she's beautiful to everyone else too,' says Sally.

'I look in the mirror and finally I can see the real me,' added Abigail.

Now, when she puts on her makeup, she knows that any glances she gets that day will be of admiration for her stunning good looks.

# Oli Watts, 23

'I've got something to tell you,' Oli Watts told his parents one stormy evening in early 1995 at their home in Suffolk in southeast England. 'You'll need to sit down.'

The dusty-haired fourteen-year-old was ridden with nerves at the daunting prospect of finally telling his mother and father the truth. But he knew it was the right thing to do.

'It's very complicated,' he said, his voice quivering. 'I've been having problems with the other kids at school.'

Oli's parents, David and Annette, sat bemused.

'What is it, son?' they asked him.

'I can't keep it in any longer,' he told them.

Suddenly, the culmination of the past four years poured out.

'I'm being bullied,' Oli said, tears welling up in his blue eyes.

He went on to describe to his parents how he had suffered continuous name-calling and humiliations in lessons.

'I don't know why they chose me,' he told them.

On one occasion, Oli was locked out of his English lesson by his tormentors. They let him back in only when they spotted their teacher approaching.

'The kids in my class flick elastic bands at me,' he went on.

Despite telling his teachers on numerous occasions, matters did not improve.

Growing up in Suffolk, Oli had always been an articulate and inquisitive child. At the age of eleven, he was ambitious beyond his years.

'I want to do lots of big things!' he told his mother one day. 'I want to change the world.'

By the time Oli was thirteen, he was already a budding businessman, thinking up a variety of madcap ideas. However, having such an overactive brain did not endear Oli to his fellow pupils at his comprehensive school in Suffolk. Most of them branded him a 'geek' and excluded him from their social circles.

Most days, Oli tried to underplay the bullying. He assumed it was a natural part of childhood. He also despised seeing himself as a victim. But the bullying had a huge mental effect on Oli.

Whereas before, he was outgoing and talkative, he started to become shy and reclusive. By the age of fourteen, he stopped going out with friends completely and spent most of his weekends at home, working on his computer.

'I was a shell of a person,' Oli now says. 'It was mostly name-calling but verbal bullying can hurt more than you might think.'

Finally telling his parents lifted a huge weight off Oli.

'Right,' said his father David. 'You're not going back there ever again'. He reassured Oli that they would find an alternative. 'We'll get you into another school. They can't hurt you any more.'

Both David and Annette felt a strong sense of guilt for not having protected their son.

'Why didn't you tell us sooner?' Annette asked.

'Because I was embarrassed,' replied Oli. 'I didn't want to have to ask for help.'

The next few days were tough for the family. Oli stayed at home while his parents alerted the school about the bullying. Within two weeks, they had secured him a place at another comprehensive in the nearby town in Essex. It was a larger school but it was well known for its strong stance against bullying.

Oli was nervous on his first day but soon discovered that it was very different.

'The staff were always very supportive,' he says. 'And I made lots of friends very quickly.'

Above all, Oli was determined not to be beaten by his tormentors. Back in his bedroom at nights, he spent hours surfing the Internet, looking for sites to help him deal with the psychological effects of being bullied.

'When I searched the Web looking for something that would connect with my feelings about being bullied, all I found were dry academic explanations,' says Oli.

It became clear that no such thing existed.

One evening, Oli was in the car with his father.

'You know you've got a ninety-pound phone bill?' David told Oli. 'It's from all those websites on the Internet you go on.'

Oli knew he would not be able to pay his father back.

'Why don't you set up your own website about bullying?' he then urged Oli.

Encouraged by his father's suggestion, Oli decided to make a positive stance against his experience of bullying.

When he finished his homework that night, Oli created a webpage and filled it with an article on bullying. Over the course of the next few days, it triggered Oli to start a site with resources on, and about, bullying. Just four months later, at the age of sixteen, Oli started his own business, a website called Pupiline.net – which eventually dissolved (see below) and the domain name is now owned by someone else.

In just nine months, he recruited a team of young people to write, design and publish a young persons' webzine, which told his story and addressed some of the key issues facing young people today. It dealt with issues such as exam stress, illness and dating.

'That's why I set up Pupiline.net, so young people would have somewhere to go, do cool stuff, put their views and ideas forward, and do loads of other top things, read about and get advice on things that are affecting people of our age everywhere,' he says.

The site boasted ten to fifteen thousand hits a month and won the backing of Prime Minister Tony Blair, the National Association of Head Teachers and the Secondary Heads' Association.

'Taking the first steps was difficult, but it's reaped some serious benefits,' he said at the time. 'We've had a lot of great responses from visitors to the site, often very touching. Helping other people overcome bullying makes me very satisfied – I'd hate other people to go through what I experienced.'

Apart from resources on bullying, the 'Issues and Advice' section contained information useful for any school-going kid – preparing for exams, what to do after you leave school and health issues such as teenage cancer and epilepsy.

The 'Features' section dealt with teenage problems such as dating, dumping, driving, finances, food, friendship, sex, part-time jobs and pregnancy. 'Cool Stuff' had links on films, music, freebies, games and all the things that teenagers love. All content came from people under the age of twenty-one.

Oli probably never imagined that a project he started to counter bullies in school would make him, at the age of sixteen, one of Britain's youngest entrepreneurs.

The site won several awards, including the Cable and Wireless Awards in 2006, Pricewaterhouse Coopers Leaders of Tomorrow and the International Childnet Awards.

Pupiline.net became bigger than anyone imagined, providing a vital service for many young people. Many schools also started using the Pupiline site to support their teaching of citizenship.

It was the anonymity of the Net that allowed Oli to present his ideas to investors without prejudice, and his experience of trying to find funding for the company spawned a pilot project that was designed to draw out teenage businesspeople. It led to the creation of a network for other entrepreneurs called Young First Tuesday.

First, Oli negotiated an initial £100 sponsorship deal with a branch of Burger King, run by a friend of his father. This allowed him to buy a domain name and to set up shop.

Using the Internet, he then signed up to a service called the First Tuesday Network, a matchmaking service that links would-be investors with entrepreneurs in the high-tech sector. He netted a number of backers. As a result, he managed to get £250,000 in funding.

Young First Tuesday, set up with the help of Steve Morton, a friend of the Watts family, is an Internet-based version of the 'grown-up' matchmaking programme.

It was a not-for-profit project aimed at the fourteen-to-nineteen age group. Steve Morton wrote to more than two hundred local schools and the response rate has been nearly 100 per cent.

Teenagers in the region started to submit business plans online. It earned Oli much media attention and praise, and even a nomination for a People's Award. Things developed at a tremendous pace. The comedian Billy Connolly described Oli as 'a genius'.

'It's hard work, but it's very exciting,' he said. 'I'm very careful that I do take time to be a teenager. I still do all the things that "normal" teenagers do.'

Oli took his GCSEs in 2006 and in September that year went to study AS-levels in English language, sociology, and information, communications and technology at Colchester Sixth-Form College.

Meanwhile, he tried to remain positive about his past.

'Whenever you put people in a competitive environment, there will be stress and people will react to it,' he says. 'We're all bad at dealing with emotional awareness. People will lash out instead of talking about it.'

In late 2004, Pupiline.net dissolved, as stated earlier.

'I just felt it had run its course,' says Oli.

But Oli was not short of other opportunities. Just a few weeks later, he was approached by the British charity, the National Society for the Prevention of Cruelty to Children (NSPCC), and was asked to speak out about bullying and young people's issues to the media.

'I was meant to engage young people,' he says.

Oli was also encouraged to help other young entrepreneurs set up their businesses.

Then in 2005, Essex University offered Oli the chance to work with their business-development department, bringing all his business contacts from Pupiline.net with him.

'It was a completely different environment, being academic, to what I was used to,' he says. 'But I really enjoyed working there.'

But in June 2006, he left his post to help the government-sponsored campaign Make Your Mark, which helps young people to make their ideas happen.

His new role was to connect all young entrepreneurs with other youngsters who want to set up a business.

'It was very rewarding,' says Oli.

Then, in August 2007, he started a new job helping a company called Bright Green, whose mission is to identify and develop the talent to shape a better world – by helping organisations with an environmental agenda recruit and retain the best people they need to grow and be agents of positive change.

## BEATING THE BULLIES

One thing is certain: Oli has definitely come a long way from being bullied, humiliated and pressurised in school.

At the age of twenty-three, this young man has had the last laugh – all by taking a simple idea and turning it into one of Britain's leading teenage sites.

The whole experience has helped Oli to rebuild his shattered confidence and has turned his own awful situation into one that has helped countless other people. He has set a precedent for young people to challenge issues and has taught adults the value of listening and accepting that they may not have all the answers.

'I wouldn't be here now if I hadn't had the experience of being bullied,' he says. 'It's made my life what it is and allowed me to talk to people on a big stage.'

Oli is a young man who stands for bright ideas and refuses to be beaten. He turned his life around and is now a successful businessman.

'The fact that I've become quite successful has really turned my life on its head,' he now says. 'It's a far better way of dealing with bullies than fighting back physically.'

Oli also believes that victims of bullying should not be afraid to get help.

'The easiest thing to do is not talk about it and to

think it's not a problem,' he says. 'But if it's something that makes you feel bad, you need to talk about it. You can always turn the situation around.'

It is a big step to stand up and fight against discrimination, but Oli's story shows how beating the bullies really can transform your life.

# Graham Mallaghan, 37

'Shh!' whispered the librarian, Graham Mallaghan, diligently trying to preserve the quiet sanctity of the library while on noise patrol.

His round baby face and chubby physique made him appear younger than his years. But the thirty-six-year-old postgraduate was in fact a very serious, hardworking man.

The married student had worked part time for three years at Kent University's Templeman Library on its Canterbury campus in southern England, while studying medieval English poetry. That day in February 2007, Graham thought he was just doing his duty as library assistant.

'Quieten down,' he hushed at a group of rowdy students in the middle section of the room.

They stopped talking immediately.

Graham then walked round to the back corner, furthest away from his desk, where another set of students were eating food and talking loudly.

'This isn't a social area,' Graham told them. 'It's for people who want some peace and quiet to work.'

The group looked at him blankly and continued speaking to one another.

'Did you not hear me?' Graham asked them.

Nobody answered him. One of the male students then opened up a packet of crisps in full view of Graham.

'You're not allowed to eat or drink in here,' Graham told him. 'Please could you throw those in the bin immediately?'

This time, the student complied with Graham and the group quietened down. Graham did not think twice about the situation – he felt confident that he was simply fulfilling his job as library assistant.

Over the course of the next five months, a large number of students were regularly threatened with fines by Graham for misbehaviour, such as noisily munching on snacks or disturbing readers by using a mobile phone. However, unbeknown to him,

Graham was becoming the butt of jokes to this group of undergraduates.

'Have you been told off by that porker in the library yet?' students would comment. 'What a righteous idiot.'

But, for one female pupil, Graham was about to go one step too far.

'Will you please quieten down?' Graham pleaded with her as she spoke on her mobile phone in the middle of the library. 'You're disrupting everyone else.'

There were important mock exams looming for third-year students and Graham wanted to ensure that there was as much peace and quiet as possible.

'Whatever,' she replied, unbothered by Graham's position of power within the library.

Graham was enraged by her indifference and lack of respect.

'If you do not turn your mobile phone off now,' he told her, 'you will be banned from the library in the future.'

The girl looked at him in disgust. Her blood boiling, she said her goodbyes to the person on the other end of the telephone line and switched off her mobile.

'There,' she told Graham sarcastically. 'Your orders have been obeyed.'

Later that evening, the female student mulled over her encounter with the young librarian. 'Who does he think he is?' she asked herself. 'What an idiot!'

The following day, she engaged a few of her friends into a discussion about Graham. It turned out that many of these students had also taken great exception to being constantly told off by Graham.

'He reckons he's something special,' a male friend laughed.

'Yeah,' another undergraduate added. 'He's always telling me off for the pettiest things.'

A few days later, while this particular set of friends studied together in the library, they were told off again by Graham for talking too loudly.

'The porker strikes again,' one young man laughed.

'We can't just let him get away with treating us like this,' a female student added. 'We've got to teach him a lesson.'

That afternoon, the group decided to wreak revenge on Graham.

'Let's really embarrass that fatty,' one of the girls whispered. 'He deserves it, pathetic little man.'

After hours of deliberating, the group, consisting of men and women, finally settled on a plan of action – one that would involve publicly ridiculing Graham.

'It's going to be hilarious!' the girl added.

That evening, back at home, one male member of the group sat down at his laptop and logged onto the social-networking website, Facebook. People use Facebook, like the other popular site MySpace, to keep up with friends, family, and work colleagues.

Facebook groups are set up on a huge range of topics and interests, and they can then be joined and contributed to by individual users.

'Umm.' He rubbed his hands together. 'This is going to be fun.'

After a few minutes, he had set up a whole page dedicated to Graham. The group were aiming to degrade him publicly.

He then downloaded a photo of Graham, which he found on the library homepage.

'What shall I write under it?' he wondered.

Just seconds later, he had come up with a tirade of abuse aimed at Graham's physical appearance and character.

Over the course of the next few days, more than 360 students at Kent University joined the group on Facebook, to post cruel jibes and messages of hate.

For weeks, Graham endured sniggering behind his back. He was also puzzled when students attempted to take pictures of him at work.

'Are you writing a piece about the library?' he asked one girl, clutching a camera.

He assumed the photos were for an article for the university newspaper.

'No,' the girl replied, sniggering. 'It's for something very different.'

Graham was bemused. But he did not suspect anything at this point.

Then, in April 2007, Graham decided to log onto a popular website a friend of his had recently joined. It was Facebook. He registered his details and sent out requests to his email contacts to join him on the site.

That lunchtime he excitedly returned to the computer room at Kent University and logged back onto the website.

'What the—' Graham gasped loudly, as his Facebook profile page loaded up.

An image of him appeared on the screen next to a link entitled 'For those who hate the little fat library man'.

He could not believe his eyes. His hands trembling, he clicked on the page link and waited for it to open. Another unflattering photo of Graham then popped up with a series of comments aimed at ridiculing him.

Graham sat transfixed as he read out the messages posted by his fellow students at Kent University. He simply could not believe that he had a whole page dedicated to insulting him. He was even more horrified to discover that one member wanted to beat him up on his way home.

'If I am given a chance before I die, I want to kick his arse. LOL [laugh out loud],' the threatening message read.

Another had launched a competition for the most amusing photographs taken of him at work without his permission.

'He is a baby man – half baby, half man. The uni is certainly ticking their equal employer boxes,' read another message.

'The man who sees all, especially when you don't want him to,' one of the profile creators added at the bottom of the page.

'Oh yes, he is the library man who goes around trying to fine people £75 for using their phone or eating!'

Another girl claimed to have taken pleasure after seeing Graham fall from his bicycle into the path of a car.

'Sadly, he managed to dive out of the way,' she wrote.

'There was a picture of me that one of them [the group members] took on his phone,' says Graham.

Graham was even more shocked to find that the

Facebook group had existed for weeks before he knew of it.

Scrolling down the page, he discovered it had been set up at the end of February 2007. It was clear to Graham that the group aimed to make a mockery of him.

'I felt betrayed and violated,' he says. 'People I thought were my friends had even put nasty messages up.'

The bullying also destroyed Graham's sense of self-worth and affected his studies.

'I was devastated. I just couldn't understand how other human beings could be so cruel,' he adds. 'It took away all my confidence.'

Graham still cannot understand why the gang pinpointed his weight as a factor.

'I have a small frame, I'm five foot seven and weigh eleven stone – that's not obese,' he says. 'I just have a beer belly, that's all.'

Graham was particularly shocked by the number of students who joined the Facebook group.

'I was on noise patrol in the library and that's going to attract some degree of ill feeling, but I thought I was just doing my job,' he said. 'I felt really angry and distressed that people wanted to stop me carrying out my job and humiliate me. It was really threatening.'

The group was finally closed down a few weeks later after the university, Graham's employer, had alerted Facebook.

A student who continued with the site when its original creators were stopped was later being investigated, along with two students who posted particularly hurtful comments.

Following the discovery of the profile, many students wrote to Graham to apologise after the section was shut down. One of them admitted, 'My behaviour was everything but mature and responsible.'

A university spokesman said, 'We have no objection to students using sites such as Facebook as long as they do so in a responsible manner. However, we draw the line at offensive, derogatory statements and will not tolerate abuse of any kind.

'Some of the comments on the website were deeply offensive and, as Graham's employer as well as his university, we alerted Facebook to this contravention of their code of practice.'

Facebook said it reserved the right to shut down offensive profiles with hateful or harmful behaviour. The website's terms of use say members may not post material that could 'intimidate or harass another'.

Meanwhile, on the Canadian version of

## BEATING THE BULLIES

Facebook, more than seven hundred people recently joined a group that targeted an allegedly homeless woman addicted to drugs, posting comments without her knowledge.

Again, as soon as it was notified, Facebook removed the profile and, at the time of writing, Canadian police are investigating whether or not to pursue criminal prosecutions.

While these are extreme examples, they are not the only ones and it certainly seems that defamatory statements made on such websites are on the increase.

The problem seems to lie in the fact that many people do not realise that posting about another person on such a site can very easily constitute a defamatory publication. A defamatory statement is simply one that lowers a person's reputation in the estimation of right-thinking members of society, or causes that person to be shunned or avoided.

Kent University is now taking disciplinary action against the four male and female first-year students who initiated Graham's Facebook profile.

Although Graham still has his own personal Facebook pages, the group targeting him is now banned from the site.

For Graham though, the lesson is clear.

'There were a lot of cutting remarks, mostly

picking on me about my appearance – which were particularly hurtful and unjust,' he says. 'I was incredibly upset at the time. But I can't just stand by and let these people abuse me and my position. Anyone thinking that it's harmless fun is wrong. These people were malicious and calculated.'

The experience of being cyberbullied may have dampened Graham's spirit for a time, but now he is determined never to let anybody degrade or intimidate him again.

'In some ways it's made me tougher,' he adds. 'I want everyone to know just how dangerous bullying over the Internet can be.'

# 20

# Jenny Souter, 22

**G**rowing up in the idyllic Scottish county of Perthshire, Jenny Souter was academic and loved going to school. When she was appointed a school prefect at Blairgowrie High in September 2002, she was delighted. She loved to set a good example for the younger children.

One cold and barren day in October, Jenny attended her classes as normal. At morning break, she put all her folders in her locker and started her prefect duties. This included controlling the common room – an area where sixth-form pupils could spend their free time.

As she opened the large, wooden door into the common room, a younger girl squeezed past Jenny and headed straight for the vending machine.

Shoving her money into the slot as fast as possible, the girl was clearly nervous and knew she was breaking the rules. Jenny marched up to her.

'You're not allowed to be here,' she told the girl. 'You'd better go or you'll get into loads of trouble.'

Some of the regulations Jenny had to implement as prefect did not always make her popular at school. But she tried hard not to scare or intimidate the younger pupils.

'Shut up, you fat bitch!' the girl suddenly replied. 'Who do you think you are?'

Jenny was shocked. Nobody had ever spoken to her like that before.

'You're going to be in a lot of trouble if you don't go,' Jenny repeated.

She hoped the girl would just leave without causing any further problems.

'Fine,' the girl sneered, as she walked off. 'You stuck-up ugly bitch'.

That last comment really hurt Jenny. Inside, she was angry and confused. She could not understand what had provoked this attack and why this girl would insult her. But it was not over yet. The next day, this girl decided to take revenge against Jenny. Over the next few weeks, she unleashed a spiteful campaign of revenge.

Three other female pupils, aged between twelve and fifteen, also joined in on the campaign.

Soon it had developed into regular verbal intimidation.

The girls even scrawled graffiti on every school wall to target Jenny.

'Fat bitch' it read.

By Christmas, the bullying was occurring on a daily basis. It was during this time that Jenny was meant to be sitting important mock exams for her three Highers, the Scottish equivalent of A-levels.

In January 2003, one of her tormentors crept up behind Jenny as she walked towards the toilet. She grabbed a bunch of her blonde hair and pulled it so hard that Jenny's neck twisted back.

'Ouch!' Jenny shouted out. 'What are you doing?' But the girl just kept tearing at her hair.

'You're gonna pay, you cow!' she muttered.

A group of Jenny's friends were outside the hall window and could see what was happening, but were too far away to help.

A few minutes later, a teacher from a nearby classroom came in and pulled the girl off Jenny. As Jenny lay in a heap on the floor, her body was shaking uncontrollably. She was due to sit an important mock exam in ten minutes' time but was rushed to the nurses instead, who told Jenny she was suffering from shock.

'They're not scared of anyone,' said Jenny.

During another incident, the gang of girls surrounded Jenny in the playground and taunted her.

'It doesn't matter what you say or do, we can still get to you,' they shouted.

Jenny managed to run away. But, by this time, the bullying was having a profound effect on her mental state.

'Jenny has always been bright and bubbly, but over the past few months she's really changed,' Jenny's best friend, Kirsty MacGregor, told Jenny's mother Glenda.

Jenny lost confidence and became frightened. She also started to have severe panic attacks and her school work suffered. Jenny was so tired that she could not concentrate and failed her maths mock exam.

'When I closed my eyes I imagined different situations and what the gang might do to me,' she said. 'I lay awake trying to work it all out and prepare myself. Then, because I was exhausted next morning, I didn't want to go to school.'

But Jenny tried to stay strong.

'The one thing that kept me going was my belief

that in the end they wouldn't win. I clung on to that,' she said.

In February 2003, Jenny was subjected to an attack in the rector's office at her school, where she had gone to seek help. The then rector, Bill Kirkpatrick, attempted to intervene, but Jenny's head was banged against a wall by one of her bullies.

After this serious incident, her family contacted a solicitor, Mike Tavendale. Jenny then went to court in Perthshire to obtain the first interdict of its kind against the gang of bullies. She claimed she had been persistently tormented by a group of younger girls for eight months.

The interdict meant if either of the two girls intimidated Jenny, or incited anyone else to bully her, she would be arrested.

Jenny's mother, Glenda, said the legal move had been supported by a large number of parents. 'Jenny's done nothing to deserve this and we had to do something about it,' she said.

Meanwhile, Perth and Kinross Council released a statement saying that the headteacher was working with the education authority to address the issue.

At the same time, the mother of one of Jenny's tormentors, who was subject to the interdict, appeared at Perth Sheriff Court to protest against the move. The twelve-year-old's mother admitted her daughter had twice been excluded from school.

'It's affecting my daughter very badly as well', she said.

This particular girl was then charged with breach of the peace.

In May 2003, Sheriff Michael Fletcher granted a non-molestation order against four girls, aged fourteen and fifteen, who were described at Perth Sheriff Court as the ringleaders. The interdict would prevent the four, who cannot be named because of their age, from physically attacking Jenny and causing her fear and distress.

Jenny's case made legal history because it was the first time an interdict had been granted against school bullies. Cameron Fyfe, a Scottish litigation lawyer said the sheriff's ruling was a legal breakthrough.

'Breaching an interdict is treated as contempt of court and the consequences can be quite severe,' he said.

In an attempt to crack down on bullying, teachers at Blairgowrie High were called to a meeting on classroom discipline. A former policeman was also appointed 'corridor discipline monitor' – a bodyguard.

Perth and Kinross's education director, George

Waddell, then said the authority was taking a firmer stance against the bullies.

Jenny said after winning her landmark judgment, 'It was very tough and at times nearly broke me. I had to learn to be brave but I'm a stronger person because of what happened. Every day, I was getting abuse and threats. I've had panic attacks and had to see my GP. Now I just want to be left in peace to get on with studying for my exams.'

Jenny returned to Blairgowrie High a few days after winning her court battle. But she was told by another pupil that her bullies wanted revenge.

Jenny was petrified.

With the backing of her parents, she chose to continue studying for her Highers at home. A source at the school told the press the latest threats against Jenny were common knowledge among pupils.

'I'm not surprised Jenny's decided to stay at home to avoid any more trouble,' he said. 'To be honest, with the exams starting in a week's time, I would be surprised to see Jenny back at all. She's had a hellish time.'

Jenny's ordeal even led the school to be dubbed 'Battlefield High'.

The case came back to Perth Sheriff Court later in 2003, when Sheriff Michael Fletcher authorised police to arrest two of the girls named in the interdict if they continued to bully Jenny.

Solicitor Mike Tavendale had told the court that the interdict should remain in place since the girls were 'out of control'.

'They have shown a complete and utter disregard for authority,' said Tavendale. 'As a result, my client has suffered greatly.'

'I only ended up taking this court action as a last resort,' Jenny said after this second hearing. Around the same time, lawyer Cameron Fyfe was approached by seven families who wanted to sue their local authorities over claims that schools have failed to stop their children being targeted by bullies.

Three of the pupils represented by Fyfe were no longer in school and one pupil had not attended classes for eight months. Fyfe said that in each case the school had been asked to take steps against the bullies but had failed to do so.

'Most children who are bullied have to come out of the school altogether and they usually have a long delay before they get another place in a different school. Their whole education suffers as a result,' he said.

Three of the cases were against Edinburgh City Council, two were against Glasgow Council and there was one each in Dundee and Aberdeen.

The pupils claimed that they were regularly kicked and punched and some were thrown against corridor walls. One overweight child was dubbed 'pig face' while another with a poor complexion was nicknamed 'pizza face'.

However, Professor Pamela Munn, director of the Anti-Bullying Network, said the quickest way to stop bullying was for the school and the education authority to take action rather than pursuing lengthy legal cases through the courts.

'It's very regrettable that the victims of bullying feel they have to go to court to resolve these issues, as we know court proceedings can take a long time and be quite protracted and very stressful for all concerned,' she said.

'The way to tackle these issues quickly is to work with the school and, if the school is unsympathetic, the next recourse is to the local authority.'

Meanwhile, it was revealed that ChildLine in Scotland, which had set up a bullying hotline to help schoolchildren, received about six thousand telephone calls that year from pupils seeking advice on how to deal with bullies at their schools.

'In terms of how schools respond to bullying, it's quite a patchy picture across Scotland,' said Anne Houston, director of the organisation. 'Some schools are managing very well and others are still saying that bullying is not an issue in their school.

'All schools, even the best, will have incidents of bullying and it's about having a mechanism to deal with that as and when it happens.'

Although the bullying destroyed her confidence, Jenny is determined to get her life back on track.

'My pride and self-esteem was being knocked every single day,' she says. 'I can't imagine how terrible it would be to be bullied if you don't have support. I've learned a lot. And the most important thing is I know that good can come out of a bad situation.

'I had terrific friends who have always been there for me and my family has been strong,' she added.

Jenny left Blairgowrie High School in June 2003 after completing her sixth form.

She is now studying behavioural sciences at the University of Abertay in Dundee and hopes eventually to become a police officer.

'It was very tough and at times it nearly broke me,' she said. 'I had to learn to be brave – I'm a stronger person because of what's happened.'

# Epilogue

The good news is that, while this book was being written, the British government announced an awareness campaign for the UK, aimed specifically at cyberbullying, which we have met several times in the cases studies above.

Schools in England will also be advised on when to confiscate mobile phones. It was technology and changes in society that had led to an increase in this type of bullying, according to the schools minister Ed Balls.

Balls was quoted on the BBC News website in September 2007 as saying, 'The vast majority of schools are safe environments to learn in. However, we know that behaviour, particularly bullying, is a key concern for parents and bullying of any kind is unacceptable.

'Cyberbullying is a particularly insidious type of bullying as it can follow young people wherever they go and the anonymity that it seemingly affords to the perpetrator can make it even more stressful for the victim.

'One message that I want to get across to young people is that bystanders can inadvertently become perpetrators – simply by passing on videos or images, they are playing a part in bullying.'

The new measures proposed by the British government have been worked out as a result of talks with other stakeholders, including mobile-phone companies, bullying experts and websites such as YouTube, MySpace and Bebo.

However, we are not there yet. And bullying, as we have seen, can destroy lives. It can change your personality and it can make you feel powerless. You may not even think of yourself as being bullied but it could be happening all around you and it can occur in many different forms.

You could be being called names, teased, pushed or pulled, have possessions taken from you, ignored or excluded, attacked because of religion, colour, sexual orientation, disability, family or financial background or have malicious rumours spread about you.

Whatever the type of bullying you are experiencing, the message is that you must not suffer in silence. In 2006, Bullying Online conducted a national survey across the UK and found that 69 per cent of pupils had experienced bullying in school. It is essential we tackle this problem before it becomes epidemic.

Bullies will pick on anyone they think is vulnerable and they will do it out of boredom or because they need to boost their ego – just as Abbi Morrall's tormentors targeted her.

Yes, they enjoy the power – they love it – and the control they have over you probably makes them feel invincible.

According to the Bullying Online charity, an average of at least 16 children kill themselves in the UK every year because they are being bullied at school and no-one in authority is doing anything to tackle the bullying in school. And a third of secondary-school children said they live in fear of going to school because of bullying, according to evidence from Dr John Balding, of the University of Exeter.

It is becoming increasingly serious, as Britain has one of the highest suicide rates in Europe. The Samaritans estimate that in the UK there is a suicide every eighty-two minutes.

The charity Depression Alliance estimates that

each year there are around nineteen thousand suicide attempts by UK adolescents, while more than 2 million children attend GPs' surgeries with some kind of psychological or emotional problem.

Each day, two people under the age of twenty-four commit suicide. The number of adults who commit suicide because of bullying, harassment and violence is unknown, but my guess is that bullying is a factor in a significant number of the overall number of suicides.

The suicide rate for 18–24-year-old males has jumped from 58 deaths per million of population in 1974 to 170 deaths per million in 1997. In October 1999, the government reported that the number of young males who commit suicide each year in the UK had doubled over the previous ten years.

In the workplace, bullying usually focuses on distorted or fabricated allegations of under-performance.

Bullying is obsessive and compulsive. The serial bully has to have someone to bully and appears to be unable to survive without a current target.

Despite the façade that such people put up, bullies have low self-confidence and low self-esteem, and thus feel insecure. Low self-esteem is a factor highlighted by all studies of bullying. Because such people are inadequate and unable to fulfil the duties and obligations of their position, they fear being revealed. This fear of exposure often borders on paranoia.

Bullies are seething with resentment, bitterness, hatred and anger, and often have wide-ranging prejudices as a vehicle for dumping their anger onto others. Bullies are driven by jealousy and envy.

Rejection is another powerful motivator of bullying. Since childhood, bullies have learned that they can avoid the unpleasant consequences of bad behaviour through the instinctive response of denial, blame and feigning victimhood.

Nowadays, children are being tormented not only in the school playground. Some are suffering twenty-four hours a day by more advanced forms of bullying, called cyberbullying. This type of bullying extends beyond the school gates and right into the victim's bedroom. Caroline Stillman was such a victim (see Chapter 7).

Cyberbullies use modern communication technology to target their victims, including threatening text and picture messages to the victim's mobile phone, and abusive messages to their computer via an instant messenger or an online chatroom.

In a survey carried out in the UK in 2005 by the children's charity NCH (National Children's

Homes), one in five youngsters admitted he or she had experienced some form of bullying or threat via email, Internet chatroom or text message.

The mobile-bullying survey also showed that 10 per cent said someone had taken a photo of them using a mobile-phone camera, which made them feel uncomfortable, embarrassed or threatened; 17 per cent believed the image had been sent to someone else; 73 per cent knew the person who bullied or threatened them; and 28 per cent did not tell anyone.

Half of all the mobile bullying happens to youngsters while they are in school or college. Of those not at school, 42 per cent received threats after 9 p.m.

'For every parent like me,' said the British Prime Minister Gordon Brown, 'there's one great fear: your children's safety. Perhaps more than any previous generation, parents now worry about that biggest school-gate fear, that they could be putting their kids into the hands of playground bullies.

'I was lucky. I went to a big, tough school but I was quite big too and no one ever tried to bully me. And if anyone tried to pick on someone else our teachers stopped them in their tracks.'

He said that in order to stop bullying, he wants to give teachers the real power – and the capacity – to pick out, stop and exclude the bullies.

'Then, from the age they start primary school, every child needs to be taught two things: the teacher is in charge, and picking on someone else is wrong,' he said. 'But, if we are to beat bullying, we must teach every young person it is unacceptable. This is a responsibility we all share.'

Workplace bullying is also on the increase but bosses are still failing to take the problem seriously, according to recent research. A survey in 2006 revealed that four out of five workers had been bullied but most had not made a complaint. The law firm Peninsula said its study of two thousand managers and thirteen hundred workers showed that bullying was a growing problem.

The findings were released in the wake of the £800,000 damages paid to a London worker, Helen Green, over bullying at Deutsche Bank (see Chapter 2).

Most of the staff surveyed by Peninsula said they had felt intimidated by a fellow worker or manager but only one in ten would complain. The poll revealed that four out of five workers had no confidence that their complaint would be treated seriously.

'This poll highlights serious concerns faced by employers regarding the growing issue of bullying in the workplace, most seriously that few employers believe their companies are suffering at the hands of bullying, yet a high percentage of employees have been victims,' said Peter Done, managing director of Peninsula.

'By taking such a stance towards bullying, employers are attempting to brush the problem under the carpet, which can have serious consequences.'

The truth is that people are generally bullied because they possess rare qualities that the bullies lack. One could almost say they should be envied – and very often they are, albeit in a destructive way.

So the moment a bully starts is the moment their target knows they must be doing something right. This is not to say that people being bullied will not at low times feel terrible hurt, loneliness and despair.

They would not be human if they did not.

But they should remember to reserve their pity for those who would hurt them – for they are to be pitied, and with pity comes contempt.

# Bullying Facts and Tips

What effects does bullying have?
• Emotional
• Loss of confidence
• Loss of self-esteem
• Lack of motivation
• Irritability or aggression
• Anxiety
• Panic attacks
• Anger/murderous feelings
• Depression
• Suicidal thoughts
• Loss of pleasure in things once enjoyed
• Loss of trust
• Sense of losing control over events or life in general
• Indecisiveness

## BEATING THE BULLIES

Physical
- Sleeplessness
- Nausea
- Sweating/shaking
- Palpitations (heart pounding)
- Lethargy (sluggish, no energy, not caring)
- Skin complaints
- Backache
- Stomach/bowel problems
- Migraine/severe headaches
- Change in appetite

Kinds of bully

Physical

Physical bullies intimidate their victims by using violence. This includes hitting, kicking and spitting, or even destroying the victim's possessions. This type of bullying is the easiest to recognise, since victims may have injuries, and seeing someone hit another child cannot be mistaken as play-fighting when it is all one-sided.

Verbal

Verbal bullying can often be worse than physical bullying, since it is easier to inflict upon peers. Name-calling, insulting and making racist remarks takes no time at all and can be done roughly anywhere. These bullies use words to hurt or humiliate their victims. It is difficult to recognise, because the scars are on the inside.

Relational
Relational bullies often try to persuade their peers to reject/exclude a certain individual from activities. This results in social isolation and makes the victim feel very alone. This kind of bullying is linked with verbal bullying and can involve the bully spreading nasty rumours about someone, persuading others not to be friends with the victim. Bullying in this form (usually with girls) can be particularly nasty, because it means the victim is isolated from their peers at a time when they need friends most.

What to do if you think you're being bullied
Tell someone – a friend, a family member, a teacher, your tutor. Practically anyone you tell can help you. They can help you develop a plan to combat the bullying and give you different ways to help you cope, as well as talking to someone to stop the bullying, and put an end to your misery.

Act confident: hold your head high, keep your shoulders back and walk straight. Don't forget eye contact, too.

Travel around in groups. Bullies are less likely to

choose people as victims who have a lot of friends. If there are more of you than of them, they are the ones who are more likely to feel victimised.

Stay in safe areas, such as those where there are lots of people, be that fellow students or teachers. Bullies are less likely to strike in these areas because of all the other people around.

Keep a bullying diary. Write down anything that happens involving the bullies. Save any threatening texts, voicemails or notes and use them as proof. When you feel strong enough to tell someone, take them with you and show them.

Don't fight back if you can help it. If they hit you, try your hardest not to strike back – it'll only worsen the situation.

Tips to beat cyberbullying

1. Don't respond to nasty or threatening emails or texts. That only encourages the bullies to send more.
2. Don't delete any messages, and make a note of the address or number they came from and the times.
3. Do tell a parent, teacher or other trusted adult what is happening.
4. Get advice on how to deal with the situation. You are not alone. Try www.stoptextbully.com.

Famous people who have been bullied
All sorts of people who are now very successful adults were bullied when they were young. It is encouraging to know that it is possible to succeed, in spite of being tormented at school:

Sir Ranulph Fiennes, polar explorer, bullied at Eton
'I was an attractive boy, and it was the norm for any boy considered a pretty boy to be wolf-whistled at. They'd sit on their window ledges above, whistling and shouting "tart, tart".

'Such remorseless nastiness squeezed every last trace of self-confidence from me. At one point, I stood on Windsor Bridge and contemplated throwing myself off.'

Kate Winslet, tormented at school because of her weight
'I became shy because I was overweight. At sixteen I was thirteen stone [82 kilos, 182 pounds] and was called "Blubber". It was pathetic and childish, but girls are so catty. It lasted for about two years.

'Eventually, I must have told my mother, and she took it up with the masters. They dealt with the situation without exposing my identity. I think that's very important today in cases of bullying.'

## BEATING THE BULLIES

Tessa Sanderson, Olympic champion javelin-thrower, subjected to racial abuse throughout her school life

'There was this boy who we used to call the cock of the school, who'd boss everyone around and push in front of the queue. The abuse was stuff like, "Hey, nigger! I'm talking to you, blacky."

'Guys would call me things like "coon" and "golliwog". In those days, golliwogs were on the jam jars and we black kids hated them.'

Tom Cruise, Hollywood actor, bullied for dyslexia

Tom Cruise had changed schools fourteen times by the time he was fifteen because his dad had moved around trying to find work. This was not the only problem – Cruise was also dyslexic and, because of moving around constantly, his social and academic life suffered immensely.

Dyslexia caused him to be bullied badly at school. He says the kids made fun of him, but the experience made him tough inside and he learned to accept ridicule. He is now a famous movie star, starring in movies such as *Top Gun*, *Vanilla Sky* and *The Last Samurai*.

# Resources and Helplines

ChildLine
ChildLine is the free and confidential 24-hour helpline for children and young people in the UK.

Freepost 1111
London
N1 0BR
(You don't need a stamp to post a letter to ChildLine at this address)
Telephone: 0800 111 (this helpline is free)
http://www.childline.org.uk

**BEATING THE BULLIES**

There 4 me

If you're between twelve and sixteen and are worried about something and need some help, There 4 me can help with issues such as abuse, bullying, exams, drugs and self harm.
http://www.there4me.com

Bullying Online

Bullying Online is the UK's leading anti-bullying charity and provides support for more than half a million people each year including families, individuals, schools and youth organisations.
http://www.bullying.co.uk

Beat Bullying

This website provides online help and advice to young people who are being bullied.
http://www.need2know.co.uk/beatbullying

Stop Text Bully

This is a charity that can help anyone who is being bullied by phone or on the Internet.
http://www.stoptextbully.com

Abs Kids
Bullied Abbi Morrall's website provides tips on how to handle bullies and where to get help.
http://www.abs-kids.co.uk

Stamp Out Bullying
This website was made to help victims of bullying or people who have been bullied in the past to encourage victims to speak out. It was set up by bully victim Sarah Costello.
http://stampoutbullying.tripod.com

Work Place Bullying
This is a nonprofit website working to provide a legal resource to those working against bullying or harassment of any kind in the workplace.
http://www.workplacebullying.co.uk.